Empty Womb, Aching Heart is a refreshingly candid account of the transformational faith journey through infertility. As the author skillfully leads the reader through agonizing encounters with the unfulfilled desire for children, she provides insight and wisdom into a growing awareness of God's grace. Surely the candor that allows the reader to capture an inside view of the continuous emotional hurdles will inspire other hurting women and men to confront their own struggles so that they, too, may discover Christ's love in the face of suffering.

> Dr. Thom Needham
> President, Global Executive Resources of San Francisco, and former Associate Dean for Marriage and Family, Graduate School of Psychology, Fuller Theological Seminary

Empty Womb, Aching Heart is a thoughtful contribution to the sensitive issues experienced by couples who are challenged by infertility. This book connects us to the lives of people who are discouraged, feel isolated, and very much alone. Their stories lift our hearts and our faith to see hope from a new or clearer perspective.

> Karen Chernekoff, MFT
> Marriage and Family Therapist,
> Laguna Niguel, California

HOPE AND HELP *for* THOSE
STRUGGLING WITH INFERTILITY

EMPTY
WOMB,
ACHING
HEART

MARLO
SCHALESKY

BETHANYHOUSE
MINNEAPOLIS, MINNESOTA

Published by Bethany House Publishers
A Ministry of Bethany Fellowship International
11400 Hampshire Avenue South
Bloomington, Minnesota 55438
www.bethanyhouse.com

Printed in the United States of America by
Bethany Press International, Bloomington, Minnesota 55438

Library of Congress Cataloging–in–publication Data

Schalesky, Marlo M., 1967–
   Empty womb, aching heart : hope and help for those struggling with infertility / by Marlo Schalesky.
     p. cm.
   ISBN 0–7642–2410–7
   1. Infertility—Psychological aspects. 2. Infertility—Religious aspects—Christianity.
I. Title.
   RC889 .S29 2001
   362.1'96692—dc21
                                                       2001001316

MARLO SCHALESKY has had over 400 articles published in a variety of Christian magazines and writes regularly for *Power for Living*. She has had two novels published, and also is a licensed minister in the Church of the Nazarene. She and her husband live near San Jose, California.

To
Madeline,
who prayed

ACKNOWLEDGMENTS

Special thanks to all those who shared their hearts, and especially to Julie Donahue for all her help.

CONTENTS

Section Four: *Struggles of the Spirit*

Section Five: *A Word of Hope*

INTRODUCTION

It wasn't supposed to be like this. Even when I was a little girl and boys had cooties, I knew that someday I'd grow up, get married, and have children. After all, didn't everyone? As I entered adulthood, everything seemed to be going along fine. I met a wonderful man, got married, and on our honeymoon we had fun discussing what we might name our future children. Later we bought a house with extra bedrooms for the kids we hoped to have soon.

But the years passed, and no children came. No morning sickness, no rounding belly, no baby showers filled with cute little booties and boxes of diapers. Soon hope turned to fear and trips to the mall changed to travels to the doctor's office. Tests and more tests, fertility drugs and ovulation sticks became a part of my everyday life. But still no babies. Fear turned to grief and pain. What was happening to all our dreams? Would there never be a baby in the nursery? A pink-cheeked child to call me Mom?

Despite the ache of longing, the world continued as it always had. My friends had children, relatives announced the arrival of new babies, mothers wiped the noses of their toddlers and sent them off to Sunday school. And there my husband and I sat, alone and lonely, sure we were the only ones in the world who were denied the joy of having children.

In those days advice was plentiful. Everyone who discovered that we were having trouble conceiving volunteered their magic cure. Our fertility specialist loaded us down with pamphlets, articles, and information on Web sites. With him, we planned the course of our medical treatment. Then we attended seminars on IVF, GIFT, ZIFT, IUI, and a host of other alphabet-soup procedures. But in spite of all the information, my heart still felt as if it were breaking every day. And no one offered hope for that—until I spoke with Sandra and discovered that I was not alone in my pain.

Eventually I met others just like Sandra, just like me, who were struggling with the same heartaches, questions, and fears. As they shared their stories over cups of coffee and glasses of lemonade, I encountered a type of wisdom and comfort I hadn't found in the reams of information I had on infertility. Theirs were stories of experience, of those who had walked the path I walked and found a glimmer of peace in the midst of it. Their understanding and insights changed me. They helped me to see through the darkness of infertility and to glimpse God as I had never seen him before.

This book is a compilation of their stories.* It is not meant to be a guidebook on infertility treatments or a manual on what to do, think, or feel. It gives no easy answers. It offers no quick cures. Rather, it comes from the hearts of fellow travelers. I pray that you'll find what you need— hope, understanding, a healing touch from God.

---

*Some names and story details have been changed to protect the privacy of those sharing.

STRUGGLES
OF THE
HEART

CRYING IN THE DIAPER AISLE

Megan, age 37

I am a reasonable woman. I don't cry at weddings or at the movies (*Titanic* didn't even do it for me). But the diaper aisle at the grocery store? Well, that's a different story. The first time it happened, it took me by surprise.

I strolled down the aisle, pushing my cart with the squeaky left wheel, while my eyes scanned the shelves for the brand of toilet paper that was on sale. It wasn't Northern, or Angel Soft. *Charmin.* Ten cents cheaper for a four-pack—double rolls! I snatched two packages from the shelf and tossed them into my cart. Then I turned, and my gaze caught sight of a baby with eyes as blue as my husband's and hair the same color as mine. She was staring at me from a package of Huggies. My hands clenched the cart handle. My throat tightened. My vision blurred.

What was happening to me? Tears pooled in my eyes and began to trickle down my cheeks. I grabbed a tissue from my purse and dashed them away, while thoughts, unbidden, unwanted, raced through my mind. *Our daughter might have looked like her. That baby could have been mine. When will God bless us with a child? Will God ever bless us? And how can I bear it if he doesn't?*

Desperately, I fought back the tears as I hurried from the diaper aisle. I glanced around, hoping no one had noticed my awkward breakdown. It was silly, crazy, unseemly to cry over a package of diapers. What was wrong with me? Maybe I hadn't gotten enough sleep last night. Maybe it was hormones. Or maybe . . . I was losing my mind. I sighed, and rolled my cart to the checkout.

The checkout clerk pulled the cart through and then looked at me. "Hey, are you all right?" One long red fingernail pointed at me as her other hand grabbed a pack of Charmin. "You don't look so good."

I managed a watery smile. "It's nothing. I'm fine. Just allergies, I guess, that's all."

"That's too bad. February's a strange time for allergies."

I didn't answer. Instead, I pulled out my credit card and swiped it through the machine. As I walked out of the store, I told myself that my experience with the Huggies was a one-time occurrence, a fluke. It wouldn't happen again. I wouldn't let it.

But it did happen again. And again. And again. When I saw a mother strolling her baby down the sidewalk outside my dining room window, when I walked past a young boy being photographed at Sears, when all the little kids paraded up to the front of the church on Sunday to sing a special song about God's love—each time those unexpected, undesired tears clogged in my throat and smeared my mascara. And every time I fought them back and wondered what was wrong with me.

My husband wondered, too. Sometimes I saw him watching me, a strange look in his eye, as I reached for the tissues that I now kept handy. I knew what he was thinking. Where was that solid-as-a-rock woman he had married? And who was this unstable, wet-cheeked woman who had replaced her?

I asked myself the same questions. But found no answers.

Tim and I had been trying to get pregnant for five years. At first, I denied there was a problem at all. I told myself that our timing was off, that I must have ovulated early, or late, this month. Somehow we just didn't "hit it" right. I assured myself that we'd get pregnant in the next couple of months, but those months passed, and still nothing. My OB/ GYN kept saying that he couldn't find anything wrong, that I was sure to get pregnant soon. But "soon" never came. Eventually we went to a specialist who diagnosed me with severe endometriosis and found that my husband's sperm were, well, less than perfect. I remembered my anger, my frustration, when I discovered that we'd been wasting our time. If only we'd started trying to conceive as soon as we were married; if only we'd gone to the clinic sooner; if only we'd sought help from the beginning. But we hadn't. And now, only now, as I began to suspect that we might never conceive, did these strange surges of grief wash over me.

And every time they did, I wondered if I'd ever feel normal again. *"God's timing is perfect,"* my friends would say. *"God knows what's best,"* my pastor assured us. *"Get a hold of yourself,"* my mother urged. *"Christians are supposed to be happy. Remember, all things work together for good to those who love the Lord!"*

Maybe they were right. Did my tears show a lack of faith? Did these sudden outbursts reveal that I wasn't trusting in God? What kind of witness was I, with my long face, and tears in the diaper aisle? I did believe that God loved me and that he was in control. Yet despite my beliefs, the tears still came at the most awkward times. And I didn't know what to do about them. Gone was the sensible woman I had always been. And in her place was a woman with emotions strong enough to raise the stock of the Kimberly-Clark Corporation.

It took lunch with Debbie, a friend who had recently lost her father, to help me to understand what was going on inside me.

We'd just finished our meal at a local café, and were sipping tea and nibbling pastries, when the conversation turned to Debbie's father.

Debbie sprinkled sugar into her tea and stirred. "I don't know what's wrong with me," she said. "I'll see a picture of Dad, or some trinket he gave me, and the tears come again. It's awful. I don't know what to do about it."

"Why do anything?" I asked. "It's normal to grieve when you've lost someone you love. A few tears are to be expected."

She shook her head. "Yeah, but it's been more than three months. I thought I'd be over the crying stage. And besides, Dad was a Christian. I know he's in heaven. Shouldn't I be happy about that?"

I poured more tea into my cup and remained silent. Somehow her words reminded me of something else, of *someone* else, but I didn't yet realize that someone was *me*.

"I know I'm supposed to be content," Debbie continued. "And I feel like I should rejoice that he's gone to be with Jesus; but, well, it still hurts. I miss him." Her voice lowered. "You know, it just feels so unchristian to cry. We're supposed to be happy. But I can't seem to help it. The tears come anyway."

I watched as Debbie's eyes became watery. She looked away. Calmly I reached across the table and laid my hand on hers. "It's okay to cry," I said. "You've lost your father. Just because he's in heaven doesn't mean it shouldn't hurt. You have to cry; it's part of the grieving process. And besides"—I paused, and squeezed her hand tighter—"even Jesus wept."

She glanced at me. "That's right, when Lazarus died."

I nodded. "Even though he knew that he was going to raise Lazarus from the dead, he still wept; he still felt grief. Crying isn't unchristian. In fact, sometimes it's right to cry."

As I drove home that day, a brightly colored ball bounced out in front of my car. I stopped as a little boy, not more than four years old, scampered after it. A little boy with his baseball cap on sideways and bright suspenders holding up his pants, a little boy so much like the son I longed to have. I blinked rapidly, fighting to hold back the tears. Then my own words came back to me: *Sometimes it's right to cry*. Were those words true, even for me?

As I thought about it, I realized that, like Debbie, I too had lost someone I loved—the child I longed for, but didn't have. Why did I think my loss was less significant, less painful? Why did I believe that I didn't need to grieve? Perhaps, like I'd told Debbie, it was okay to cry. After all, I reminded myself, even Jesus wept.

All this time I'd been fighting the tears and telling myself I should trust God and be content, I hadn't allowed myself to grieve. I thought crying was a sign of weak faith, but maybe it was a sign of God's attempt to bring healing to my heart. If that were the case, I needed to stop fighting the grief and accept it, just as Jesus accepted it. I needed to allow the tears to cleanse me. I needed to switch to waterproof mascara.

These days I cry when I need to cry, without feeling guilty. And lately I've discovered that as I allow myself to fully experience grief, the tears come less often. I can look at the baby on a box of Huggies and I can listen to the children sing at church without having to dig in my purse for a tissue. But if the tears do come, I don't try to stop them. I've come to realize that God understands my tears, and that they don't fall to the ground unnoticed.

Infertility is a hard road, a painful road. Sometimes tears are needed to smooth the way. Sometimes it's right to cry.

TWO

BABIES, BABIES EVERYWHERE

Melissa, age 31

It had been a hard day anyway. That time of month started again, crushing the wisps of hope I'd been foolish enough to nurture. Despite daily shots of Pergonal and seemingly endless trips to the infertility clinic, and despite the intrauterine insemination performed just two weeks before, I wasn't pregnant. Again. Still.

So, as the sun began to slip over the horizon, all I really wanted to do was forget—forget about cradles and bibs, diapers and rattles, anything and everything that had to do with the baby I couldn't seem to have.

But life conspired against me. With a tissue in one hand and the TV remote in the other, I plopped onto the couch to watch my favorite show. *Click, click.* I flipped to channel 3, and there before me popped a cute, cooing baby. I stared blankly into innocent blue eyes set above cotton-candy pink cheeks, while a happy mother told me why Luvs were better than any other diaper. Quickly I switched the station. But there, a baby giggled at me from the center of a Michelin tire. My thumb pressed hard on the remote again. *Entertainment Tonight.* Surely this program would be safe. I settled back into the couch as Mary Hart introduced a new John Travolta movie. In a moment Travolta himself smiled from the screen, and . . . I caught my breath . . . there in his arms was a smiling baby boy. I felt my heart tighten. Not again! Was the whole world against me? I shut off the TV and tossed the remote on the coffee table. It was bad enough to have my hopes crushed yet again, but to endure the constant reminder of my pain was just too much to bear.

It would have been easier if that night's experience had been unusual. But, unfortunately, it seemed that wherever I went I was confronted with happy parents enjoying their beautiful children. During trips to the store, I watched hurrying mothers push restless toddlers in carts. At church, families gathered at the altar to pray, the children's small heads bowed over folded hands. Even driving down the street wasn't safe. There, moms pushed strollers to the corner playground, and kids buzzed around in the sand like a hundred brightly colored bees. Even at work, I was constantly confronted with pictures of Mom, Dad, and baby smiling from brass frames, children's first school photos, a daughter's prom picture, or a son's graduation photo—all experiences I would never enjoy. And now even Hollywood contrived to remind me of my loss.

I rubbed the tissue over my eyes and pulled myself from the couch. One thing I was sure of, I needed a break.

"Honey!" I called to my husband in the other room. "Get me out of here."

He peeked around the corner. "What's the matter? I thought you were watching that weepy angel show."

"Take me to dinner. Now."

Tom raised an eyebrow. "What's up?"

I crumpled my tissue and threw it in the trash. "I've just got to get away from all these babies."

"Babies?" He glanced around the room, then looked at me as if I'd lost my mind.

I motioned toward the TV. "Every channel has babies on it," I muttered, then proceeded to tell him what had happened.

He nodded. "A little Mexican food will cheer you up. San Juan Bautista? I know it's your favorite."

I brightened. "It's not too late to drive that far?"

Tom grinned. "You can drown your sorrows in a vat of hot salsa. C'mon." He grabbed his coat and headed toward the door.

I sniffed, and followed him.

In forty-five minutes we pulled up in front of the tiny Mexican restaurant in the small mission town of San Juan Bautista. I glanced around at the empty parking lot and sighed with relief. A quiet meal in my favorite restaurant was just what I needed. And it looked like that was what I was going to get.

Tom helped me from the car, and we entered the restaurant hand in hand. Soon we were seated, and within minutes we'd ordered our favorite meals.

I smiled and looked around me. The setting was perfect. Gentle music drifted over the speakers. A candle flickered on the table. And best of all, we were the only customers in the whole restaurant.

Tom cleared his throat, dumped a teaspoon of sugar into his iced tea, and stirred. I recognized his frown as one he wore whenever he was thinking about how to say something he wasn't sure I'd like. Finally he glanced up at me. "You know, children aren't going to go away. Wherever you go, you're bound to see babies, or at least kids. You can't bury your sorrows in salsa every night."

I avoided his eyes. "I know."

"You're going to have to learn to deal with it. You can't keep letting the sight of a baby throw you into a tailspin."

I dipped a tortilla chip into the salsa bowl.

Tom stopped stirring.

An awkward silence fell between us.

Finally I spoke. "The problem is, I don't know how to deal with it."

Tom opened his mouth to respond, but stopped as he watched the hostess lead another couple to a table directly across from us. "I can't believe it," Tom said in a hoarse whisper. "Don't look now."

"What?"

He looked at the other guests and shook his head.

I followed his gaze. "Oh no," I sighed. There between the husband and wife, in a car seat, was a brand-new baby. Of all the people who could have come to the restaurant, of all the tables where they could have been seated, a couple with a new baby had to be sitting directly across from me. Just where I couldn't help but see them. It was too strange to be a simple coincidence. It was God.

Apparently Tom agreed. A sympathetic smile crossed his lips as his gaze returned to me. "Well, it's official," he murmured. "Looks like God wants you to face this head on."

I grimaced. "But I don't want to."

"I don't think you have a choice."

"Okay, then, how do I find joy in a world filled with children who are not my own?"

Tom didn't answer.

The baby's sharp cry broke through my thoughts. I turned to see her little red face bunch up as another wail escaped her tiny mouth. A moment later her mother looked as if she, too, were going to burst into tears. The woman turned to her husband and whispered loudly, "I told you this would never work. We can't go anywhere anymore." Her voice sounded desperate.

Her husband scowled. "Is she hungry?"

"I *just* fed her."

"What about her diaper?"

"I changed it."

"Gas?"

"How am *I* supposed to know?"

With each exchange, their voices grew louder, and so did the baby's cry. Finally the woman slammed down her menu, grabbed the car seat, and rushed toward the door. Her husband watched her go, then slowly set down his own menu, shook his head, and followed her.

As I observed the scene, a lump grew in my throat. "Those people don't know how lucky they are."

Tom's eyes narrowed as he looked at me. A full thirty seconds passed before he spoke. "It's kind of sad, isn't it?"

I nodded. "It's downright absurd. You and I understand better than anyone what a miracle a child is. Yet people like that have no idea how blessed they are. They have children, and we don't. That's more than sad."

"That's not exactly what I meant. I didn't mean we should be sad for *us*."

"Who, then?"

"I was sad for them."

"What?!" My eyebrows shot up.

Tom remained calm. "Don't you think it's sad that those people have a baby but they don't seem to be enjoying her, at least not right now? We should pray for them."

"Pray for *them*?!" My voice raised an octave as a hundred objections flew through my mind. I was the one who needed prayer. I was the one hurting. I was the one denied the miracle that those people enjoyed. I was the one that Tom should feel sorry for! *I, I, I* . . . the pattern of my thoughts struck me and left me breathless. I was thinking only of myself, my own pain, my own loss. And, come to think of it, it was the same every time I saw a baby or a child. My thoughts consistently turned to myself. My eyes invariably looked inward. Now, in a flash of understanding, I saw that this habit had done nothing but increase my pain.

What if, for a change, the sight of a baby caused my vision to turn outward instead? What if I took Tom's advice and prayed for the parents of the children I saw? What if I prayed for the kids themselves?

I decided to try it. After all, it couldn't hurt. And maybe it would help me, too.

"Okay, let's do it," I said.

He smiled, and I began forcing the words out: "Lord, please help those parents to rely on you as they raise their baby. Help them to know what a miracle a baby is and to enjoy every minute with her, even when she's crying. Strengthen them and give them wisdom in the days and years ahead. Be close to them as they make decisions that will affect the little life in their care. And bless the child, Lord." I paused, unable to go on.

Tom took up the prayer. "May she grow up to know you and love you. Protect her as she encounters the evils of this world. Make yourself known to her. Amen." A hand reached across the table to squeeze mine. "I think we've found your answer," Tom said, "or at least part of it."

I managed a weak smile. "Maybe we have."

Since that day, every time I see a baby or a child, every time I feel the grief rising in my chest, I stop and offer a prayer for the parents and the child. Sometimes the prayer is only one sentence, and other times it lasts a few minutes, but always it asks for God's grace and love to fill the family.

I'd like to say that these prayers completely cured my feelings of pain and sorrow when confronted with babies, happy families, and reminders of children. But the truth is, it still hurts. It just doesn't hurt quite as much. Somehow the small act of prayer helps. Maybe because it enables me, just for a moment, to see past my pain and into the heart of God. And that is a vision even more powerful than the sight of a precious child.

THREE

MONTHLY CYCLE, MONTHLY TEARS

Colleen, age 36

I never thought this would happen to me. I had it all planned out. Kevin and I would graduate from college, I would work for four years, and then we'd start our family. We'd have three, maybe four kids before I reached the age of thirty-four. Then everything would be right in my world.

But thirty-four has come and gone, and nothing is like I had planned. Infertility, I have found, is a journey within a journey. The larger journey takes a lifetime. Mine started when I was a little girl and Aunt Mae gave me my first doll. The path was bright then, filled with marigold dreams and wishes on daisies. The path continued through my young adult life as I met and married Kevin and my mom started talking about what it would be like to be called "Grandma." I looked ahead and saw a bright future. The road dipped and curved, and though I couldn't see it all, I knew there would be good days ahead. But then the clouds came. Not the white fluffy kind, but gray, somber rain clouds that darkened my path with doubts and discouragement. The darkness grew thicker as the years passed and no children came. Rain, in the form of tears, muddied my walk. And I wondered, *How could this happen to me? Where does this dark path lead?*

I've yet to find all the answers. But today I have to find a way to live through the smaller journey, the monthly journey. It always starts the same, with that insidious whisper of hope. *Could this be the month? Could I be pregnant?* Every twinge is analyzed. I feel a little pain, and I wonder if it means something. My stomach flutters, and I think that it's morning sickness. I press my hand against my belly and close my eyes. Is a new life growing in there? Could it be? No, I mustn't think about it. I can't get my hopes up again. Resolutely I turn away these thoughts. I try to forget. But I can't. I count the days. Twenty-six, twenty-seven, twenty-eight. I hold my breath. Twenty-nine, I release it. Thirty. Two days late. Thirty-one. This is it! Thirty-two. Then the bleeding starts. And my heart breaks . . . again.

You'd think I'd get used to the ache. You'd think after so many months, I'd learn to be tough, to ignore the frustration, to live with the pain. But I never do. Every time it hurts the same. Every time I wonder how I can live through another month on this endless roller coaster of hope and disappointment.

So I sit and tell myself not to cry. I say I shouldn't be surprised. But I cry anyway. I close the bedroom door. I don't want Kevin to hear me. I don't want him to know that I'm crying again. I don't want him to know that I've failed one more time.

Despite the closed door, I hear him in the kitchen fixing himself something to eat. Has he heard me crying?

I wrap my arms around myself and look out the window. Storm clouds gather in the sky—gray, dark, and depressing. The wind moans and the sound pierces my heart. Outside, the bottlebrush tree sways and a spattering of rain shimmers down the windowpane, obscuring my view. The weather matches my mood. Every month it's the same: hope and disappointment chase each other in countless loops along the path of my life. How I hate it! And I wonder, *Will I ever feel normal again?*

I hear my husband leave the kitchen and I grab a tissue to cover the tears. But it's too late. My eyes are already swollen, and my nose is red.

As soon as Kevin sees me, he knows. He always knows. For a full minute, it seems, he stands in the doorway, not knowing if he should come in and try to comfort me or just turn around and walk out.

"Not this month, huh?" he mutters.

I say nothing.

Slowly he leaves the bedroom and returns to the kitchen. In the silence I feel the loneliness, the longing that never seems to be fulfilled. Why do I go through this every month? Will the pain never end?

I smooth the patchwork quilt on our bed. It was made by my grandmother—an heirloom, something to be passed down from generation to generation.

Then a shaft of light, bright and warm, slices through the clouds to illuminate a rose pattern on the quilt. In the distance, beyond the storm, a rainbow arches through the sky. The brilliant colors make me think. I catch my breath and remember God's promise in the Bible to never flood the world again. Is there a promise here for me, too?

"You got a postcard from your Aunt Mae," Kevin calls from the hall. He walks in to hand me the card. *Are you okay?* his eyes ask.

I'll survive, mine say back.

I reach for the card and see that it is actually a photo with writing on the back. Aunt Mae is visiting a Peruvian village. Some kind of huge snake is draped around her shoulders, and she's wearing a canvas hat and khaki shorts. She stands with an arm around a dark-skinned girl. The girl's smile is contagious, and I smile back. Then I focus on the image of my favorite aunt. Fifty years old and never married, Aunt Mae is the unpredictable, adventurous one in our family. And I love her for it. The last time I heard from her, she had just left the Brazilian jungle. Now she'd made it to the mountains of Peru—all in pursuit of the will of God.

I turn to the writing on the back. *This is Nina*, it says. *Her parents were killed last year. I've decided to bring her home with me. The papers are all signed. We'll arrive in the States at the end of June, so plan for a visit in early July. Love and hugs, Aunt Mae.* Then, in smaller print at the bottom, it reads, *Who would have thought I'd be playing "Mom" after all these years? God's sense of humor, I guess. Or maybe it's just his love.*

I pause at the last line and am reminded of the rainbow—God's promise of love, his promise that the sun will shine again. He kept that promise in Aunt Mae's life, despite all the disappointments that have darkened her path—the death of her fiancé, the loss of her dreams. Maybe if God brought her through the dark and into the light, he would do the same in my life.

I stand and rest my elbows on the windowsill, the photo clutched in my hand. Outside, it is still dark and dreary. But in the distance, there is a break in the clouds. As I live through the storm of infertility, the way is dark. But somewhere out there, the rains will cease and the sun will break through. Someday all this will be behind me. And God has promised that he will never leave me nor forsake me.

Yet in the months to come I know the tears will flow again. I can't suppress them; I can't ignore them. But I can raise my head, look for the rainbow, and remember that every month is another step closer to the light. One more step on the larger journey.

For now, I can only look ahead to the future and learn to see my disappointment against the backdrop of eternity. I must tell myself to keep my eyes not on today's pain but on the eternal goal of a life lived in a way worthy of Christ, who calls me his own. And whether that life has biological children, adopted children, or no children at all, I know that it won't be wasted.

So for today I choose to place my hope not in children but in him, despite the darkness, despite the rain. Today I will remember the rainbow.

"Blessed be the name of God forever and ever. . . . He changes the times and the seasons. . . . He knows what is in the darkness, and light dwells with Him" (Daniel 2:20–22 NKJV).

FOUR

SLAYING THE DRAGONS OF DESPAIR

Kate, age 40

MAY 12

Dear God,

Have you lost your mind? I think I'm losing mine. How could you do this to me? You created me with such a strong desire for children and then made me unable to have them. Is this some kind of cruel trick? Are you playing a game with me, a game in which I'm always the loser? That's the only explanation I can find to what has happened, despite the $14,000 we paid for in vitro fertilization. I thought for sure this IVF cycle would work. I thought you would certainly give us a child this time. After all, I've prayed so diligently, believed in your power, had faith when hope seemed as faint as smoke on the wind. But now I don't know if I can do this anymore. I don't know if I can still believe, still hope, when this pain weighs so heavily in my heart *that I know I'll be crushed beneath it. IVF was so expensive, Lord, paid for with money we'd scraped together from relatives, borrowed from our credit cards, and taken from the bit of savings we'd gathered over the past eight years. And now it's come to nothing. Nothing. A word that describes my life. Where have you gone, God? What is this terrible thing that is happening to me? How can I live through this pain?*

I looked back over the words I had written six months earlier and realized that nothing had changed. After two more unsuccessful IVF attempts, things had only gotten worse. We were broke. We were tired. And we were still barren. All our hopes, all our desires had evaporated in the haze of failure. I was ready to throw in the towel not only on treatments but on life. I picked up my pen and wrote again.

NOVEMBER 20

Terrible thoughts are coming to my mind. Frightening thoughts. If I were out of the way, Jay could find another wife, a fertile wife. If I had an accident, maybe the life insurance would pay off the debts we've accrued from all these useless IVF treatments. What is the point of living, God, if you won't grant me a child? I can't bear this feeling of ever-empty arms. Is there any worth to this fruitless life I'm living? I am a withered tree. I am a plowed field, but without seed. I am an empty jar, without purpose. I have forgotten what it means to really live.

I laid my journal down and glanced out the window. A leafless birch swayed in the wind, its white branches scraping the windowpane. Silently I watched. The same cold scratching echoed in my heart.

For months I'd been stumbling through life not knowing where to go, what to do next. It seemed that all my time and energy were consumed with endless trips to the hospital, doctor appointments, evenings hoping against hope that this might be the month.

The normal life I had once lived had somehow turned into this constant stress of treatments, disappointments, and pain. Nothing was the same as before we'd started on the journey of infertility. Mostly *I* wasn't the same. I didn't go to my book club anymore. I no longer felt like playing racquetball at lunchtime. I didn't think I could afford to waste money on membership at the health club. Every penny had to be saved in case we needed to do another cycle of IVF. And recently Jay and I had even quit the couples group we'd been going to. I was just too tired, too stressed from treatments to consider doing anything else.

What had happened to me? How could I get back to the normal, happy person I'd once been?

There was a quiet knock at the door before it opened. "Are you okay in there?" Jay called as he stepped into the room.

"No," I answered.

He looked at me. I looked at him. Neither of us spoke. We didn't need to. I recognized his worried gaze; I'd seen it a hundred times over these last months. I could sense his helplessness, his inability to figure out how to help me. It surrounded him like a thick cloud. But I couldn't blame him for that. I didn't know how to help me, either.

Minutes passed in the heavy silence. Quietly I closed my journal and slipped it into a drawer. Still Jay didn't say anything, and neither did I. There had been a lot of silence between us these last years. Silence that grew in proportion to my despair.

The telephone rang and Jay hurried to get it. "It's Janet," he called. "Do you want to talk to her?"

I didn't feel like talking to anybody. But Janet was a good friend. Jay handed me the phone.

"Hey, what's up?"

"A painting class, that's what!" Janet's voice was full of excitement. "Just like we've always talked about. Are you up to it?"

"Uh, I don't know. When is it?"

"Thursday nights at the college. Come on, let's do it. It'll be fun."

Fun. There was something I hadn't experienced in a long time. "How much does it cost?"

"Nothing. I'm paying for you. I know how much you've always wanted to do this. Consider it an early birthday present."

I almost said no, and then thought, *Why not? Maybe it's time I did something just for me, something that had nothing to do with trying to get pregnant.*

"Okay," I said. "I'll do it."

"You won't regret it," Janet assured me. "I'll pick you up next Thursday at six-thirty. Wear old clothes."

I smiled into the phone. "Okay."

A week later Janet and I walked into a large auditorium filled with easels, tables, paints, and brushes. We slipped into our painting smocks and found places next to each other near the back. As the class began, Janet grinned and waved her brush at me. "Here we go," she whispered. "Move over, Monet, here come Kate and Janet!"

For the next couple of hours I swirled colors onto a canvas and it felt like I was spreading balm on my wounds.

Janet looked over at my rendition of a bowl of fruit and giggled. "Is that green thing a pear, or what?"

"Of course it's a pear! I thought it looked pretty good for a first try." I glanced at her painting. "Yours looks less like a pear than mine!"

"Aw, you're just jealous." Suddenly she turned and swabbed my white smock with a blotch of red paint.

I whirled and touched her nose with my green brush before she could react. "This is not a face painting class!" she shrieked.

The instructor's voice boomed across the room. "Ladies! Please keep your paint on the canvas."

Janet and I looked at each other and broke up in laughter like children. I was beginning to remember what it felt like to be normal. It was a good feeling.

That night as I lay in bed staring at the shadows on the ceiling, I wasn't thinking of my need for a child; I was thinking of my need for a life. For once I wasn't begging God for a baby or planning what I would do if we failed another IVF cycle. I wasn't debating about adoption or thinking about baby names. Instead, I was considering all the things I would like to do with my life. I had allowed myself to put everything on hold. But I wasn't going to do that any longer. I needed to stop living for the tomorrow that might never come and start living for today. Infertility had nearly consumed my life. It was time to reclaim it. It was time to remember how to live again.

The next week I began playing racquetball at lunch hour, just like I used to do. I put in for a new position at work. I volunteered to teach aqua aerobics at the YMCA. And, of course, I continued to take the painting class with Janet. As I started to live again, I noticed that with each passing day life got a little bit better. Even though I still longed for a child, even though we continued pursuing treatments, the feelings of hopelessness, of despair, subsided.

Later, Jay and I decided to adopt. When we finally got our child, she became part of my life rather than all of it. Working through my despair had taught me that my life was precious. I needed to enjoy each moment; I needed to live each day to the fullest, as God intended.

Today I can look back and see that infertility made me a better woman. It made me a better mother. Somehow, through the pain, God had made a river in my wasteland. He showed me how to live.

FIVE

THE MISERY OF MOTHER'S DAY

Michelle, age 33

It was the Sunday I hated most of the whole year. I almost stayed home, pleading sickness. I wanted to roll over in bed and pull the covers over my head in tight denial, just as I had done in years past. But it never helped. Besides, this year my husband hadn't been able to wriggle out of his church duties. And if he showed up without me, there were sure to be questions, followed by murmurs of pity and trite advice. So I had put on my most comfortable dress, lifted my chin, and decided to grin and bear it.

Now as I stood just outside the sanctuary, I wondered if I had made the right choice. Could I get through the singing without bawling and drawing unwanted attention to myself? Could I sit and smile pleasantly when the mothers were honored? How could I possibly endure the whole service without a mascara disaster?

With trembling hands I clutched my Bible to my chest until my knuckles turned white. Then I stepped from the foyer into the sanctuary.

Spring dresses and scrubbed-pink children met my gaze. I closed my eyes. Around me, snippets of muted conversation reached me as the music leader played softly at the piano. I paused to allow the quiet notes of "Great Is Thy Faithfulness" to wash over me.

"Are you really faithful, Lord? Even today?" I whispered. I felt goose bumps rise on my arms and a lump form in my throat.

With a sigh I opened my eyes. I didn't need to look at the bulletin to know what it would say right up front: "Happy Mother's Day." For me, there was nothing happy about it.

I took a few steps forward and could smell the roses even before I saw them. I tried not to look, but that only made it worse. There was a huge vase at the front of the church filled with dozens of beautiful long-stemmed pink roses. Their velvety petals shimmered with tiny drops of dew. One rose for each mother in the congregation.

Of course, I wouldn't receive one, because I was childless. As hard as my husband and I had tried, and as much as we had prayed, I still wasn't pregnant. So month after month, year after year, we planned and waited and hoped. And still Mother's Day came and went, leaving me with the same hollow feeling inside. I didn't think this year would be any different.

Quickly I slipped into a side pew, as far from the front as possible, and dropped my head. Before I could stop it, all the insensitive comments I'd ever heard came drifting through my mind. *"By the time I was your age, I already had five children." "Well, God knows best. Maybe he knows some reason why you shouldn't be a mother." "How long have you been married? And you don't have any children yet?" "What's wrong? Don't you like kids?" "Why don't you adopt?"*

Chills ran up and down my arms as I tried to listen to the chorus being played and to think of the words: "Thou changest not, Thy compassions they fail not."

Compassion? Where's your compassion for me today, Lord? It's the same every year. Pastor will call all the mothers to come forward, and I'll be left sitting here with all the men and children. Then I'll have to listen to another sermon on the joys of motherhood. I really don't think I can bear it.

Bryan came in and sat beside me. He reached over and laid his hand on mine. I blinked back unshed tears.

Then Bryan made his way to the front of the church to join the worship team. After a few songs, our pastor stepped to the pulpit with a huge smile on his face. "Will all the mothers come up front, please?"

Here we go again. I tried to act natural as dozens of women in their spring dresses rose from their seats and stepped toward the altar. I looked around to confirm my fears—just me and the men and children . . . but wait a minute!

There, to my right and in the next section of seats, sat a little old lady with white hair. It was Dora. I knew her. Why hadn't I noticed that she never went up front on Mother's Day? Could it be that she was childless, too?

I moved to the edge of my seat to get a better look. I could see that she held her head high and even managed to smile as the pastor handed a rose to each mother. Even as the women came back down the aisle, Dora had a look of contentment and joy.

As the pastor announced a Mother's Day potluck following the service, I studied her. I recalled countless times when she had stood and praised God for his love and faithfulness in her life. She told about the tough times as well as the good, how he had helped her through the Depression era and through the death of her husband, and how he had healed her when she was in the hospital. I could see now the thread of joy that had held her life together—even though she must never have had children. How did she manage Mother's Day so well?

When the time came to greet one another, I hurried toward Dora. She turned and smiled at me, her hand extended.

"How do you do it?" I asked.

Her smile broadened as if she knew just what I meant. "It will always be hard, dear," she said as she patted my arm. "You never get over the wishing." Her voice softened. "But for today, let God be enough."

"Enough?"

Dora paused and looked me directly in the eye. "Enough to love."

I frowned. *What is she talking about?*

The music started up again, and I returned to my seat.

Enough to love. The strange words haunted me. *I don't understand,* I shouted silently to God. *What does it mean?* No answer came except the words to the hymn that was being sung by the congregation: "My Jesus I love Thee, I know Thou art mine."

The verse swept through me, probing, beckoning, bringing the smallest hint of understanding. It was true that I didn't have children, but I did have Jesus. I knew he was mine. And despite my pain, my grief, my anger, I did love him. I really did. So maybe, for this moment, for this day, he was enough.

The last line of the verse stirred me and I found myself singing, too. "If ever I loved Thee, my Jesus, 'tis now."

Yes, I love you now, I thought, *now when my heart hurts so much I think it will break, when the reminder of what I may never have is all around me, now when I can't ignore the fact that you haven't answered my dearest prayer. Now, Lord, I want you to know that I really do love you, in spite of it all.*

As the second verse neared its end I sang the final line even louder. "If ever I loved Thee, my Jesus, 'tis now!" And this time it was as if I could hear the echo of God's voice through mine—only a word was changed: "If ever I loved Thee, *my child,* 'tis now."

Then the tears came freely and my mascara ran down my cheeks. But I didn't care. These weren't tears of grief, but tears of understanding. When all the country was honoring mothers, Jesus remembered me. He took special note of me in my pain, in my sorrow, in my longing. I was not forgotten. The same Jesus who cared for the weak and downtrodden cared for me, especially today. Especially on Mother's Day.

As if hearing my thoughts, Dora turned and lavished her beautiful smile on me. I felt my own face lift in return, and I knew that from that moment on, I would view Mother's Day differently. It would always be hard. The pain and longing would always be with me, and I'd probably still cry sometimes when the women came down the aisle with their roses. But from now on Mother's Day would also be a special time to remember God's love for me, and mine for him.

And for this day especially, it would be enough.

STRUGGLES OF THE MIND

I'm Pregnant, You're Not

Carol, age 36

I needed a vacation. Just a little time to get away from the pressures of infertility and a chance to finish recovering from the miscarriage I had had several months before. I thought a trip to my favorite resort in Mexico would be a perfect way to refresh my soul. So my husband and I packed our bags, jumped in our car, and headed for the border. But first, we decided to make a quick stop at my sister Carla's house. Little did I know how that stop would change everything for me.

As we walked in the door, I saw my sister lying on the couch looking awful. Her face was pale (no makeup), her normally tidy hair a mess. It was almost noon and she was still in her pajamas.

"Come on in," she moaned.

I tossed my purse on a chair and went to her. "What's wrong?" I asked. "Is it another bout of bronchitis—or the flu?"

Her response was quick and harsh. "No, I'm pregnant, and my life is over! I'm so sick I can't keep anything down."

My heart almost broke. *Pregnant? My baby sister?*

Carla and Brent were newlyweds and had planned to wait five years before starting their family, in order to be better established. She had a great teaching position, which she'd have to give up, and she explained how hard it was dealing with such an abrupt change in their lives.

Still, hearing her displeasure about being pregnant was like a slap in the face. On the outside, I tried to act excited and thrilled for them, while inside I was all torn up. As I sat next to her on the couch, I kept praying, *Lord, please help me not to cry.* He did help me to control the tears, and I wanted to say, *"Carla, God has chosen to bless you with this gift of a child. I know it wasn't in your plans just yet, but he has better plans for you and Brent. This is a gift from him."*

But before I could say the words out loud, the Spirit of God spoke to me: *"Carol, I have chosen to bless you with this gift of infertility. I know it wasn't in your plans, but I have something better for you. Accept it from me."* I was dumb struck. How could I argue with that? Yet the hurt in my heart was still there.

As Carla went through her pregnancy and passed safely beyond the point where I had miscarried, I had to constantly fight jealousy and anger at God for giving her what she didn't want right now, while *not* giving us what we had desperately desired for so long. Carla was great about keeping me up to date on how she was doing. She called me after her doctor's appointments and let me know how much weight she'd gained and how strong the baby's heartbeat was. When I saw her, she would let me feel the baby kick and ask my opinion on how to decorate the nursery. But to me it was all a reminder of what I didn't have and maybe never would. My husband and I visited and watched as Brent rubbed Carla's abdomen and talked to the baby. I looked at my husband and died inside knowing that I was unable to give him the same pleasure.

It seemed that every aspect of Carla's pregnancy was another arrow piercing my heart. Even watching my parents' excitement was like a kick in the shins. *We* weren't able to give them a grandchild. I felt inadequate, deficient. I can't begin to count all the times I coveted my sister's child.

On the day of delivery, Brent called us to let us know they were leaving for the hospital. We live three and a half hours away, but we told them we'd be down as soon as possible. After clearing our schedule for the next five days, we again jumped in our car and headed south. I guess I assumed she would want me there since I was her only sister and we had casually talked about it earlier. But to be honest, nothing was going to keep me away. I knew it would be painful for me, but this could be the closest I would ever come to having a baby of my own.

As we went through the day of labor and I held her hand and tried to encourage her, my husband and I realized it was going to be an even harder day than we had first thought. Our baby, the one I had miscarried, would have been born exactly one year previous.

Ellie arrived at 9:21 P.M. As I stood there watching my new niece squirm in her mother's arms, my heart was divided between elation for Carla and Brent, love for Ellie, and the pain of the emptiness I felt.

After everyone else had had a chance to hold the baby, it was my turn. I stepped out into the hallway with her and let the tears flow freely. She was so precious and tiny and vulnerable, her little face still red from the trauma of birth. I wanted to be able to protect her, but she was not mine. "I'm your Auntie Carol," I whispered.

She looked up at me with eyes bright and innocent, as if she had come straight from heaven just an hour before. So I asked her if she had seen her cousin Chris (the name we had given our baby) up there, and if I could kiss her since I never had a chance to kiss him.

God had graciously cleared the hallway for this time alone, but it was too short—a lifetime too short. This sweet child had to go back to the parents whom God had chosen for her, and they would be the ones to love her and care for her.

Sometimes, even now, when I look back at my sister's pregnancy, the tears still come to my eyes. I'm not sure if it's just "that time of the month," when emotions run high, or if it's reliving the pain of "I'm pregnant, you're not."

As time goes by, however, and we enjoy visits with their family, we hurt less and less as we watch Brent, Carla, and Ellie grow as a family. Carla and Brent are wonderful parents, who desire to bring up their daughter to know and love God, and they are doing a fantastic job. Ellie is six months old now and thriving on the love of her mommy and daddy. She couldn't be in a better home.

And best of all, her auntie and uncle get to love her up when we visit. She gives the best kisses, grabbing your hair on both sides of your face and pulling it right into her open mouth. It's a slobbery one, but what a thrill to get a kiss like that. And what a joy to see her receiving love and giving it freely. Knowing that she, Carla, and Brent are so happy makes me think that just maybe God knows what he's doing after all. It reminds me that his plans, even when they're difficult to accept, are much greater than our own. It helps me to trust him even on this painful journey called infertility.

Of course, it's much harder to watch babies in the arms of unloving parents who will bring those children up in an environment where God is not welcome. I still wonder why God gives children to them rather than to us. That will be one of my questions for the Father when I get to heaven. But for now, I can only trust his wisdom.

For me, the biological time clock keeps ticking. My hope grows dimmer each month. Yet we are grateful to the Lord for his grace to make it through each time of disappointment. We remind ourselves that God has a bigger plan and a larger picture than what we can see. We will trust his hand and rest in his grace, no matter what tomorrow brings or doesn't bring.

SEVEN

"JUST RELAX, DEAR," AND OTHER MADDENING ADVICE

Nancy, age 29

I tried to keep our fertility problems a secret, but somehow the news leaked out. And worse yet, Mildred heard about it. That morning she scooted from the senior Sunday school class and made a beeline straight for me. If I'd known what was coming, I would have hidden in the women's rest room, but it was too late. Mildred had her sensors honed in on me, and now there was no escape. She came toward me with her wide-brimmed hat askew on her head and her big black King James Bible tucked under her arm.

My eyes widened. I clutched my small NIV New Testament to my chest as if it would protect me. I glanced around the foyer, but no one was around to rescue me. Then came the assault.

"Oh, Nancy, I hear you're having trouble getting pregnant," Mildred spoke in a voice loud enough for anyone to hear in the next room. "Is it true, dear?"

"Well, um, yes," I mumbled. I tried to think of a reason to excuse myself, but it was no use. Mildred would not be stopped.

"It's all right, honey," she clucked. "You're just too uptight." She patted me on the arm. "Don't you worry. Just relax, and everything will work out." She smiled sweetly.

Relaxing will open my blocked fallopian tubes? I thought. I bit my tongue and said nothing.

"Yes, I'm sure that's the problem," she continued. "You're too tense. A nice vacation is all you need. A little trip to Florida or somewhere, and you'll have a bun in the oven in no time. Why, that's just how it was when I got pregnant with Paulie. I'll never forget that trip. . . ."

I sighed as Mildred launched into a long story about how she conceived her son while on her honeymoon. Apparently Clarence had taken her all the way to Florida, and nine months later little Paulie made his appearance. So, all I needed to do was relax, take a vacation, and *poof!* a baby would show up in about nine months.

I stood there clutching my New Testament while Mildred continued to diagnose my problem. Finally Dolores approached. I started to inch away, hoping Mildred would be distracted by Dolores. No such luck.

"What a lovely morning it is," Dolores commented.

Mildred turned toward her, and I started to step backward, but Mildred's hand came down on my arm before I could make my move.

"We were just talking about having babies," Mildred told Dolores. "Did you know that Nancy is having trouble getting pregnant? Isn't that a shame?"

Dolores's wary blue eyes examined me from head to toe.

I shifted nervously from one foot to the other.

"Humph." Dolores adjusted the dial on her hearing aid. "You're young yet, dearie. There's plenty of time for children."

I was beginning to feel warm, but before I could respond, a group of women emerged from a classroom and headed our way. Mildred motioned for them to join us. "Camille, didn't your niece have trouble getting pregnant?" she asked a tall woman in the group.

Camille nodded. "Yes. She adopted a little girl, and then she was pregnant with twins two months later. She's got three kids under two years old now. What a zoo!"

Mildred squeezed my arm tighter as she turned back to me. "See there, honey? Maybe you should adopt."

Camille glanced at me. "It worked for Cindy. Have you thought about adoption?"

"Uh," I hesitated, not wanting to share our private thoughts and plans with a near stranger.

"My aunt said you should stand on your head," a younger woman piped in. "That's supposed to help you get pregnant. Have you tried it?"

I didn't even attempt to answer that one.

"That's silly," another woman said.

The younger woman tossed her head back. "It's worth a try. I know I'd try anything if I couldn't have a baby."

I felt my jaw tighten as my polite smile turned into a grimace. But the torture session wasn't over yet.

"Have you done in vitro fertilization? My sister's friend did that and got pregnant within a year," offered a woman I'd never met. "You should think about it."

"That test tube stuff is immoral!" Mildred spouted. "Having children is in God's hands."

Dolores nodded in agreement. She again seemed to size me up with her gaze. "God knows who should be a mother and who shouldn't." She paused and her eyes narrowed. "Maybe God knows you wouldn't be a good mother. Not everyone's cut out for the job, you know."

My face flushed. "That's the most—"

Mildred cut me off. "Now, now, dear, God knows best."

Before I could say anything more, music drifted out from the sanctuary, and the women headed inside, leaving me alone in the foyer.

I stood there for a few minutes contemplating all they had said. And the more I thought about it, the angrier I became. *Of all the rude, insensitive, prying . . .* , I fumed.

"Are you all right?" My husband stepped up behind me.

I whirled around. "Oh . . . sure," I stammered.

Jeff's brows tightened. "What's wrong?"

A sarcastic smile crossed my lips. "Apparently nothing standing on my head can't cure," I quipped.

Jeff smiled. "Well, that's a new one."

"Or maybe I'm just too tense." I mimicked Mildred's tone.

His grin broadened. "Okay, I'd have to agree with that, at least for the moment."

"If we take a trip to Florida, though, I'm sure to get pregnant. Guaranteed."

"Ah," Jeff gave a knowing nod. "So that's what this is all about. You've been getting advice from Mildred."

"Her and everyone else on the planet. How did you know?"

He laughed. "I got the Florida suggestion earlier this morning."

"Ugh. Can you believe it?"

Jeff put his arm around my shoulders. "Come on, hon, you can't worry about what those old ladies have to say."

"I don't . . . but I do!" I groaned. "It just gets hard to hear. And the unsolicited advice would be more palatable if it only came once in a while, but lately it seems like everyone has a miracle cure." I shook my head. "You wouldn't believe how many times I've heard, 'Just relax.' Last week someone told me to try meditation. It worked for her sister. A woman at the pharmacy thought it necessary to tell me that stress causes infertility. Ann Landers says so."

"Well, if Ann says so . . ." my husband drawled.

I punched him in the arm. "Look out! I'm not in the mood."

Jeff rubbed his arm. "Wow! Was their advice that bad?"

I couldn't help but grin at him. "Yes. And with my luck, the next person will be your mother."

Jeff put his hands in the air in mock horror. "Whoa. That could be hard to take."

"You wouldn't tease if you'd heard how awful those women were."

"People can be pretty insensitive. But why let it bother you? Just ignore it."

"It's not that easy."

"Why?"

I thought for a moment. "I guess it's just hard when no one understands."

Jeff's voice softened. "You must admit you don't share your needs with anyone. It's hard for people to know how to help."

"I don't want help. And I certainly don't want to announce our problems to the world."

"Of course not. But what about Brenda? She cares about you. She'd understand."

I shook my head. "All she does is avoid the subject. If she does bring it up, it's to tell me about how someone got pregnant after ten years of trying."

"That's because she doesn't know what to say. You've got to tell her and others who are close to you how they can show they care. They can't read your mind. Even I can't do that."

I put my arms around him and squeezed gently. "Sure you can," I whispered. "Let's go in to the service."

Later that week Brenda stopped by to pick up some materials for our Wednesday night Bible study.

"Hey, how are you doing?" she asked.

And this time, instead of my usual "Fine, thank you," I decided to take Jeff's advice. "Well, to tell you the truth," I said, "I have some infertility tests tomorrow that I'm kind of nervous about."

Brenda tossed her keys on the table and looked me in the eye. "Would you like to talk about it? I don't have to be anywhere for another hour."

I hesitated, then nodded. "Yeah, I think I would. How about a cup of tea?"

Brenda and I walked into the kitchen, and I put the water on to boil. Then I proceeded to share with her all about the tests, my concerns, and my fears. And to my surprise, Jeff was right. She did care, and she did understand.

"Wow! This infertility thing is harder than I thought. What can I do to help?"

"Be there for me. Listen to me. It takes a load off my mind just talking about it with someone. I don't think I need more *advice*, just more understanding."

Brenda giggled. "I hear Mildred got to you."

"Not just her. I had a regular interrogation on Sunday."

"How awful! Is it hard when people ask you questions?"

"No, not people I'm close to, people who know me. For example, I appreciate it when you care enough to ask me how it's going. But I can't say that I like to tell strangers about my private life."

Brenda poured hot water over the tea bag in her mug. "No kidding. I wonder why some of those ladies think they need to offer their advice."

"I guess they're only trying to be helpful, but some of it is a little ridiculous." I recounted the entire story, from Mildred's advice to relax and take a trip, to Dolores's "bad mother" theory. As I did, I discovered that it really *was* kind of funny. In retrospect, I was able to laugh about their comments.

Brenda finished her tea and set her mug in the sink. "Well, I gotta run. Kyle's waiting for me to pick him up at the gym." She headed for the door, and I followed. When she got there, she turned back and gave me a quick hug. "Don't forget to stand on your head on your way to Florida," she quipped.

I chuckled as I watched her get into her car and drive away. Standing there, I realized the sting of Sunday's encounter had been dissolved by Brenda's friendship, understanding, and laughter. And suddenly I felt a little better.

In the following weeks and months I discovered that sharing my needs, hurts, and concerns with those closest to me lessened the impact of insensitive words spoken by others. Instead of silently steaming when someone dumped unwanted advice on me, I began to say things like "Thanks for your advice, I'll be sure to mention it to my doctor." Or sometimes I'd make a joke of it. "So that's what we've been doing wrong all this time!"

I also joined a support group on the Internet, where I found compassion and good advice from others who were going through the same pain that I was. Their wisdom and understanding have been like a balm to my heart.

Of course, I still receive plenty of prying questions and rude comments. But insensitive words don't upset me as much anymore, because I know there are people who do understand. I know I am not alone. And that has made all the difference.

EIGHT

MARRIAGE: HOW COULD HE STILL LOVE ME?

Becky, age 40

Infertility is an insidious monster. It sneaks up on you, taking a bite here, a nibble there. It feeds on your life and on your relationships.

For a long time I didn't recognize the monster. But one day I saw it—in my reflection in the dresser mirror. There it was, staring back at me through the dullness in my eyes, the stress lines around my mouth, the droop of my cheeks. I hadn't always looked like that.

My eye caught a photo on the dresser. My husband and I grinned from the silver frame. John's arms were looped around my shoulders in a casual embrace. Behind us, the ornate doors of Notre Dame rose to the top of the picture. Paris. It had been beautiful that May. And we were two young lovers walking its streets hand in hand as we celebrated our first anniversary. We were so happy then. Innocent, in love, and looking forward to a future filled with the promise of giggling children and vacations that would take us to Disneyland instead of Paris. Those were the good days. I could see it in the shine of my eyes, hear it in the laughter that would spill from my lips a moment after the camera shutter clicked. I could remember how easily John and I use to laugh together, how he would tease me when I wanted to take just one more photo. I would chuckle and skip away from him to ask yet another stranger to snap our picture. But that was BI—Before Infertility—and those days were gone.

I sighed and traced my finger over the image of my face in the picture. I seemed so vibrant, so alive, so different from the way I felt now. I looked again into the mirror. Who was this woman?

Gone was the beautiful young wife my husband married. Instead, I felt like a baby-making machine that didn't work. As a result our love life had become sterile and mechanical. The purpose of intimacy was no longer to share our love, but to produce a baby; not to enjoy each other, but to accomplish a goal. We scheduled our time together based on the reading of an ovulation predictor stick and according to the instructions given by our doctor. On the magic day when the stick read positive, I would call my husband and say, "Today's the day," and later that evening, whether we felt like it or not, we would do our "duty," our thoughts focused on the baby we hoped to conceive. No more romance, no more spontaneity, no more passion.

Slowly I turned from the dresser mirror, walked downstairs, and pulled a photo album from beneath the coffee table. I sat on the couch and flipped through its pages. Photo after photo revealed the joy of our life together: John making a face at me from behind a glass of sparkling cider. Me grinning from the top of a tall boulder, where I had climbed during a summer hike. The two of us dancing at a friend's wedding. A snapshot of me, hair rumpled, sipping a cup of coffee at the breakfast table.

As I looked at the pictures, I realized that it wasn't only our love that had changed; our daily interaction was also affected by the infertility beast. Once I had been a normal, even-tempered woman. But the monster had nibbled away at me, leaving a person who constantly teetered on the brink of anger or tears. When John was late for our appointment at the infertility clinic, I accused him of not caring. When he tried to tease me like he used to, I called him callous. When he said it would be okay if we never had children, I burst into tears and refused to speak to him for days. In my sane moments, I knew he was doing his best to understand me. But somehow it just wasn't enough.

As I sat there studying the difference between the woman in the photos and the one in the mirror, the thoughts I'd been fighting for months flooded through my mind. John should have married someone else. He could have had a family by now. How could he still love me? Did he regret saying "I do" so many years ago? Could we ever recapture the love we once had? Would we ever feel normal again?

It seemed like every week that passed, every month that proved I still wasn't pregnant, the monster grew stronger. Every day it consumed a little more of the love between John and me. Somehow we had forgotten each other in this pain-filled journey through infertility. We'd forgotten how to really see each other, to rejoice in what we loved about the other. Instead, we had become so focused on the goal of having a baby that we were blind to everything else.

We needed a change. I needed a change. Somewhere inside, an attractive, fun-loving woman was hiding. I just had to find a way to let her out again.

A week later, when the ovulation stick read positive, I was determined to make things different. That night I dressed in my best black velvet gown, did up my hair, carefully put on my makeup, and wore the special sapphire earrings my husband had given me three years before. I bought a bottle of wild new perfume and dabbed it on my wrists and behind my ears. Then I looked in the mirror and smiled. It was a forced smile at first, but at least it was a start, a beginning to recapturing the woman of fun and romance that I'd once been.

As the first stars started to peek from the evening sky, I set up our back patio table with a tablecloth, candlesticks, and our best china. My husband's favorite meal was bubbling in the oven and light music drifted from the stereo in the family room when John arrived home. I still remember the look of surprise on his face.

"What's the occasion?" he said.

I lifted my chin and offered the smile I had practiced earlier. "Because I love you, and I love us," I replied. "Tonight we're celebrating each other."

John raised an eyebrow. "Are you sure you're my wife?"

I grinned and pointed to the camera I'd placed on the table. "How many pictures do I have to take to convince you?"

He laughed. "Oh, only a hundred or so."

I picked up the camera and snapped his picture. "Now go up and change your clothes and hurry back. It's a date night."

"Whatever you say." He jogged upstairs to our bedroom while I finished preparing the meal.

As we sat down to homemade lasagna and glasses of sparkling cider, I realized something. I felt attractive again. I felt alive. And I noticed how handsome my husband was, more so than the day we were married.

For the next hour we talked and laughed and reminisced about our favorite memories as a couple. Then when we'd finished our meal, John stood and extended a hand toward me. "Care to dance, m'lady?"

I nodded and placed my hand in his. There, under the moonlight, we danced with my cheek on his shoulder and his mouth near my ear.

"We're going to make it through all this, you know," he whispered.

And for that moment, I believed him. Beneath the stars, with my husband's arms around me, the monster of infertility grew weaker, until I thought we might be able to survive the pain, disappointment, and sorrow—if only we could remember to love each other.

After that night, we planned a special date night whenever the ovulation stick read positive. The next month John brought me roses and took me to my favorite restaurant. The following month we snuggled in front of the fireplace and roasted marshmallows over the glowing coals. They were simple things, but they reminded us to listen to each other and to care. These dates soon became times we cherished, as we focused on appreciating each other, on listening to one another, and on hearing the other's heart. In doing so, they took the pressure away from performance, away from the goal of producing a baby, and instead gave us time to pay special attention to our relationship.

To my surprise, after a few months we began to find it easier to enjoy each other during the "regular" times, like doing yard work together or washing the cars or folding clothes. Soon, we found ourselves planning more trips together. With the expense of infertility treatments, we didn't have the money for vacations to Paris anymore, but we could take a walk on the beach, or see a funny movie, or take a drive to the country to watch the sunset. On Saturday afternoons we started to enjoy picnics in the park like we had in our college days before we were married—anything to help us remember how to laugh again, to remind us why we fell in love.

I'll admit the pressure of trying to have a baby still haunts us, and sometimes I feel the monster still nibbling at my heart. But now I know that at least once a month John and I will tell each other how much we love the other, and we'll take time to laugh together like we used to. And for that one day the monster will be held at bay. For that moment, at least, I know I'll be able to remember the woman God made me to be, the woman who once smiled into a camera in front of the Cathedral of Notre Dame.

NINE

MARRIAGE: NOTHING I DO HELPS

Michael, age 36

I gripped the steering wheel, clenched my teeth, and turned the ignition key in my Ford F150. *Sput, sput, vroooom.* I smiled as the engine began to purr like a contented tiger. Four hours under the hood had paid off. The truck was as good as new. I sat back and wiped an oily hand across my forehead. Who needed those guys at the repair shop? After all, I was Mr. Fix-It, an engineer, a problem-solver. And right now, after hours of being up to my elbows in grease and machinery, I felt like I could fix anything.

I sauntered into the garage and began to scrub my hands with a coarse cleanser. A dozen other things needed to be repaired today. There was the bathroom faucet, the loose leg on the dining room chair, and that squeaky brake on Shannon's mountain bike. Or maybe I should tackle the problem with the sliding door lock. I rubbed my hands together.

Today would be a good day. Nothing made me feel better than getting in there and making things work.

After a moment's thought, I decided to attack the faucet. I gathered my tools and headed toward the bathroom. A leaky faucet would be no match for me today. I opened the door, hiked up my pants, and dropped to one knee to begin clearing out the stuff under the sink. No sooner did I get my wrench onto the pipe than I heard the sound of sobbing coming from the other room. *Oh no*, I thought. *Not again.*

I knew what it was before I reached the master bathroom. As I pushed open the door, I could see my wife sitting on the edge of the tub in the bathroom. When I went in to see what the trouble was, I saw a pregnancy test stick lying on the counter. I knew from experience it was negative—again. I closed my eyes and prayed for strength. We had been so sure that this would be the month. Disappointment rose in my throat. Quickly I suppressed the feeling. I had to be the strong one. I had to fix this problem.

This month had been the third time we'd undergone intrauterine insemination. We had planned to try it only three times. The doctor had told us that if IUI didn't work in the first three tries, it probably wouldn't work at all. Now we'd have to consider IVF, a procedure we couldn't afford.

I stood there for what seemed a long time, staring at the pregnancy test, my mind racing. I had to make this better. I needed to figure out what to do.

"This isn't the end of the world," I commented lamely.

My wife didn't even look at me. She only answered by crying harder.

"Maybe the test is wrong."

"I t-tried it twice," she sobbed.

"Maybe the doctor blew it," I suggested. "I think we should try another clinic."

"*Nooooo*," Shannon wailed.

I ran my fingers through my hair and paced back and forth. "Okay, then, maybe we should try one more time. Or maybe we could get a loan for an IVF."

"It's no use," Shannon cried. "Nothing's ever going to work. We're never going to have a baby."

"That's silly," I replied in my most matter-of-fact tone. "Of course we are. If we have to go to the ends of the earth, we'll make this work."

Shannon glared up at me. "This is not like one of your broken-down cars, Michael. You can't just turn a wrench and make it work. Don't you understand?"

She stormed out of the room without a backward glance. What was wrong with her? Didn't she see that I was trying to help? Whatever I said always seemed to backfire. For five years we had traveled this rocky path called infertility. And in all that time I felt we'd made no progress. We were no closer to understanding why we couldn't conceive. The doctors didn't give us straight answers—only possibilities and statistical probabilities. No matter how much I studied the subject, no matter how many Web sites I visited, I couldn't seem to find a logical series of steps toward our goal of starting a family.

And lately when I talked with Shannon about the subject, our conversations always ended in turmoil. Nothing I said helped. I tried to be positive. I tried to suggest solutions I thought might work, but it only seemed to make her angry. It just didn't make sense. *She* didn't make sense.

Of course, I realized that the whole treatment process was more difficult for her. After all, I wasn't the one constantly being poked and prodded. But it wasn't easy for me, either. Still, at every step in the process I tried to be the rock—the one who took the positive side. My objectivity seemed helpful at first, but these days even my most reasonable suggestions were met with tears.

Infertility ought to be like a Ford F150, I thought. Then I could fix it. If I could just find the right tools, turn the proper bolts, replace the correct parts, everything would work again, just as it should.

For at least an hour I sat in the bathroom and searched for answers. But nothing came to me. Maybe Shannon was right. IUI would probably never work, and where could we even hope to find the money for more expensive procedures, procedures that weren't guaranteed to work any better than the IUI? What if this problem could never be fixed? What would I do then?

My stomach tightened at the thought. I decided to return to the guest bathroom, where life made sense. With a wrench in my hand, I knew what to do to make things right.

The next week dragged by. We went about our business without saying two words about the problem. I came home from work and fixed things. She buried herself in her work and in her spare time read her favorite novels again and again.

That week I fixed just about everything that needed fixing and more. I organized my garage and designed a new shelving system. I made the sprinkler system more efficient and gave the dogs two baths. But nothing helped. Repairing a bathroom faucet didn't fix my wife's broken heart. Redesigning a sprinkler system couldn't erase the pain I saw in her eyes. But what else could I do? She wouldn't let me help her. She wouldn't listen to my advice.

Since working around the house didn't solve our problems, I decided to take a short trip. My friend Pete had been bugging me to go duck hunting with him. But Shannon and I had been so immersed in infertility treatments that I hadn't considered going. Until now.

Duck hunting can be truly exciting—when the birds are flying. I could often shoot off two or three boxes of shells in one day. But slow days afforded plenty of time for reflection. Too much time. This particular day was dark with fog, perfect duck hunting weather—wet and cold. We set out our decoys and settled down out of sight, just in time for the opening shoot at 6:56 A.M.

As the fog bank around us became illuminated by the first morning light, we searched the sky. But no ducks appeared. So we began to blow on our duck calls, hoping to attract the birds flying above the fog. Still no ducks. The precious first moments of the day slipped by without sighting one bird. At this rate, it was going to be a long, dull day. Or so I thought.

Pete and I stood hidden in the reeds for the next two hours with our feet immersed in near-freezing pond water. My neoprene waders kept the water out, but I wished that I'd worn woolen socks. Pete, a wise man and a member of our church board for as long as I could remember, was not much for conversation. But it was he who broke the silence: "Why did you decide to come with me this weekend?"

"Oh, I just wanted to get away for a little while," I sighed.

Pete looked at me for a moment.

I shifted uncomfortably.

Finally he spoke again: "So how are you and Shannon doing with that infertility stuff?"

"Humph," I grunted. "Don't ask."

Pete nodded. "Seems to me like conception is a lot like duck hunting. The conditions may seem right. You can set out your decoys and blow your duck calls. But there's nothing you can do to make the birds come in. Must be hard, especially for you."

Pete's analogy was pretty good. He was right, of course. I couldn't fix our infertility problems any more than I could make the ducks fly. And that left me feeling frustrated and confused. "So what do I do? If I can't fix the problem, why even try?"

Pete answered with one simple phrase. It rings in my ears even now, even though he said it under his breath: "Sounds kind of selfish."

At first I had no idea what he was talking about. But a cold duck pond has a way of enabling self-reflection. As the hours passed I continued to think about Pete's comment. I didn't ask him about it. Nor did he offer any explanation. But my thoughts turned to Shannon.

Maybe all my attempts to solve the problem were for my own benefit. My concerns were centered on the fact that I couldn't do much to help the process or to alter my feelings of helplessness. But what about Shannon? What did she need from me? Apparently she didn't need my poorly conceived solutions or my attempts to try to figure out how to make everything all right. Mr. Fix-It just wasn't helpful. But she did need something from me. She needed someone to stand with her in this.

My thoughts turned again to duck hunting. On days like today, when I couldn't bring the birds in, I didn't stomp off angry and give up. I waited. I hunched down in the reeds, watched, and listened. I was patient. I was hopeful. I was ready for action.

Maybe that's how I needed to be with our infertility situation. Maybe I just needed to *be with her*, wait with her, sit quietly beside her and listen to her pain. Maybe all she needed was to know that I cared.

I cleared my throat. "Hey, man," I said. "I think I need to go home now."

Pete nodded. "I understand."

The trip home was the longest eighty miles I'd ever driven. I didn't waste any time getting into the house. I don't remember specifically what I said to her, but it went something like this: "Shannon, please forgive me for being so selfish. I truly don't know how to fix our infertility problem. I can't fix it. But one thing I do promise: I will be with you through it all. And I love you more than anything."

Tears sprang to Shannon's eyes. "I don't need you to try to fix it," she said. "All I want is for you to be there when I'm hurting. All I need is for you to understand."

I took her in my arms and kissed her forehead. "It's a deal," I whispered.

That day I learned that sometimes what I call doing nothing is doing something in Shannon's eyes. Sometimes all I can do is take her in my arms and say, "I understand and I love you." Sometimes all she needs is my shoulder to cry on.

As the months and years wear on, infertility hasn't become easier for us. Nor have we found any simple solutions. We're still putting out our decoys and blowing on our duck calls. But one thing is different. We're now able to love and support each other through this difficult process as we wait to see whether "a bird will fly overhead."

TEN

CAN WE BE A REAL FAMILY?

Sonya, age 38

"O come all ye faithful, joyful and triumphant," sang the children's choir from the front of the church. I felt anything but joyful or triumphant. Despite the Christmas lights glittering from the sanctuary's ceiling and the candles that flickered and glowed from behind the pulpit, darkness hung over me like a heavy cloak. Everything around me seemed so perfect—parents snapping pictures from the pews, Pastor Mike grinning from his chair at the side of the platform, little Mary Lou shyly stepping forward to read Isaiah 9. But of all the little girls pulling restlessly at prim velvet dresses, and of all the little boys standing tall and proud behind starched shirts and clip-on ties, none were mine. No little eyes searched the crowd for me, no little fingers attempted a wave in my direction, and no little voice called me "Mommy."

The Bible would call me "barren," a cold, empty word. I hated it, not so much because it described the condition of my womb, but because it revealed the feelings of my heart—especially at Christmastime, when families gathered, mothers baked sugar cookies, and children counted the days until they would sit in front of gift-laden Christmas trees and open presents from Mom and Dad. *Barren*—the word haunted me now as I sat in the back pew and wished for the hundredth time that Christmas didn't hurt so much. But it did. Christmas, it seemed, was a time for families. And Joe and I, with only our two dogs, did not constitute a real family. At least I didn't think so. And neither, it seemed, did anyone else. "When are you two going to start a family?" was a question we heard all too often. At our church, being "family-friendly" meant having events that focused on children. When our pastor spoke of ministering to families, he didn't mean to people like Joe and me; he meant to couples with children. In a hundred little ways those around us, and society at large, told us what we had was not enough. We needed children to be complete. Without them, our lives would forever be empty. We would never know the joy of being a legitimate family.

I sighed and closed my eyes, wishing I could block out the sound of singing voices reminding me of what I longed for but couldn't have. "Joy to the world!" they caroled in tones that expressed their exuberance. To me, it felt like a knife in my heart. Joy was for those who had children. And I didn't have any. What chance did I have for real joy? What hope did Christmas hold for people like me?

In a moment clapping resounded in the sanctuary as the kids' choir finished their final song. With sweeping bows and stifled giggles, the children scampered to a wide box in front of the pulpit and pulled from it sprigs of mistletoe tied with bright red ribbons. My throat closed as each child trotted toward their parents and presented them with the mistletoe. *I never should have come tonight,* I told myself again. But my husband ran the sound system for the performance, and no one would have understood if he had come alone. So there I sat, uncomfortable and hurting while the laughter of happy families echoed around me.

"M-Mrs. Brown?" a timid voice asked beside me.

I looked up to see eight-year-old Caroline holding out her sprig of mistletoe toward me. I quickly glanced around and noticed that Caroline's parents hadn't come tonight. In fact, they rarely came. My eyes met hers, and she smiled at me.

"Merry Christmas," she whispered, then leaned over and kissed my cheek. "I hope Jesus brings you lots of presents this year." With that, she turned and hurried toward the back door.

A strange mixture of sorrow and warmth flooded my heart. "Thank you," I choked, too quiet for her to hear me as she slipped out of sight.

There in my lap lay the small gift, the Christmas lights reflecting off the red ribbon. It was such a simple thing, so plain and unexpected. As simple, perhaps, as a baby wrapped in rags, lying in a feeding trough. As plain as the Son of God, born not before family and friends but in a stable full of animals—a gift announced not to the movers and shakers of Bethlehem, but to a few Gentiles in the East and a bunch of poor sheepherders working the night shift.

I picked up my gift of mistletoe and held it close to my heart. If animals, shepherds, and even foreign kings were remembered at the first Christmas, maybe the childless, the outcast, and the hurting were remembered this Christmas.

Perhaps God was telling me that joy at Christmas was not only for those who had children. For in Jesus there are no outcasts. Christ was born for people like me, who through the simple gift of Christ are welcomed into the family of God. So why didn't that feel like enough? Why did I still cringe when the very next day someone asked me again, "When are you going to start a family?" Why did the question still hurt?

The issue of family continued to haunt me over the next several months—through the children's Easter program, Mother's Day, Father's Day, church barbecues, and other "family" days, until one Sunday I was asked to teach the middle-grade Sunday school class. God had a surprise in store for me.

I waited, materials in hand, while Caroline and a half dozen others scampered into the classroom. A plethora of eager questions tumbled from their lips as they hurried to take their seats.

"What's the lesson today?"

"Do we hafta sing a song?"

"Are we making something?"

"How come I never get to sit by the teacher?"

I smiled and began to flip through the lesson. "Today we're learning about the sixth day of creation, how God made Adam and Eve," I informed them.

The kids rolled their eyes and groaned. They'd heard the story a hundred times before, and so had I. But that was the lesson for the day, so I began. As I read the story from the Bible, the kids interpreted it on a large piece of butcher paper taped to the table. Soon strangely colored animals, insects, and two people with heads too large for their bodies romped beneath bright green leaves in the Garden of Eden. I finished the story and closed my Bible.

"Who's this?" I asked, pointing to the drawing of a stick figure with a long beard.

Joey, who had drawn the man, sat up straighter. "That's Adam."

"Very good. And who's this?" I pointed to the figure with long hair turned up at the ends.

Caroline smiled. "Eve. She has brown hair, just like yours."

"And what do you like best about God's creation?" I asked the class.

They called out a dozen answers: "The lions!" "The birds!" "The kittens!" "The butterflies!"

"The spiders!" shouted a boy as he stuck out his tongue at the girl three seats over.

"All of this God called 'very good,'" I reminded them, "then he rested."

Caroline raised her hand. "Was he all finished?"

"All done," clamored the boy who had mentioned the spiders.

Caroline looked to me for assurance. I nodded my head. "The Bible says that God had finished his work, so he rested on the seventh day."

Caroline had a forlorn look on her face. "So there was nothing missing?"

"Nope. God had made everything that Adam and Eve needed. Creation was complete."

An awkward silence fell over the room as the kids shifted in their chairs, waiting to see if Caroline would be bold enough to ask more questions. She looked puzzled and chewed on her lip for about ten seconds. Finally she raised her head and blurted out, "But there aren't any children!"

I opened my mouth, then shut it again, staring at the kids' drawing one more time. No children, not yet . . . and still God had called it "very good." Not "almost good" or "okay" or "good-but-it-would-be-better-if . . ." After he made man and woman, he proclaimed his work finished. It was complete. They were complete. What did that mean for me? What did it mean for my view of the family?

I stumbled through the rest of the lesson with the import of Caroline's observation pounding through my heart. *Complete, even without children.* Could it be?

Later that day I sat in the swing on my front porch with my Bible open to Genesis. Suddenly I smiled. *It's true, really true,* I thought. *Joe and I are a real family, a complete family, just like Adam and Eve were.* Children wouldn't make us a family; they would only expand the one we already had.

So how could we stop seeing ourselves as a couple waiting to become a family and instead start being a family of two? Surprisingly, part of the answer came the following Christmas. I reminded myself that Christmas was a time for families—even families of two. So that year Joe and I decided to begin establishing traditions for the two of us. Instead of my decorating the tree while he sat on the couch and watched TV, we began to decorate together, just as my family had done when I was a child. Together we sipped hot cider as we strung popcorn onto long threads, hung our stockings on the mantel, and listened to Nat King Cole sing about chestnuts roasting on an open fire. And like the tradition in Joe's family, we chose to make his grandmother's special sugar cutout cookies and decorate them for neighbors and friends. Over the years these traditions have affirmed that Joe and I really are a family, not just a couple without kids.

Of course, I still long for the children I hope God will someday give us, but it helps lessen the pain to realize that Joe and I (and our dogs) are a legitimate family, after all. God looks at us and says, "very good." And maybe, in spite of my persistent desire for children, I can agree.

So these days whenever someone asks, "So when are you going to start a family?" I answer them, "We already have. We just aren't sure if God is going to add to it or not." And though that answer often baffles them, to me it has become a reminder of the grace of God.

STRUGGLES OF THE BODY

ELEVEN

MISCARRIAGE: WHEN NIGHTMARES COME TRUE

Laura, age 31

I awoke with a surge of fear. My hands, balled into tight fists, gripped the sheets as my breathing came in ragged gasps. The chill of the predawn air wrapped cold fingers around my chest and throat. I squeezed my eyes shut, then opened them again. I could just see the dim outline of my dresser and chair. The bed felt damp beneath me. Was it just a dream?

I could hear the pounding of my pulse in my ears. *Oh God, my baby!* The words shot through me as I sought to distinguish reality from the image of a miscarriage still vivid in my mind.

My husband rolled over and sat up as he mumbled, "Are you all right?"

When my mind cleared, I let out a long breath. *It wasn't real,* I told myself. *It was just a dream.* "It's nothing," I murmured. "Go back to sleep."

I pulled the covers up to my chin and waited for Rob's steady breathing. Slowly it came, the sound like gentle lapping of waves on the sand. I wrapped my arms around myself and stared at the ceiling fan whirling slowly overhead. *Surely God wouldn't allow anything to happen to this baby*, I thought. After all, we had been trying to get pregnant for almost four years. It had been a roller coaster ride of emotions—hope, and fear, and disappointment like a rush of wind through our hearts. Then, nine months ago, I had undergone surgery to widen a "tight spot" at the bottom of my uterus. The doctor said I'd have about a year to get pregnant before the opening tightened again. With the end of the year nearing, we found out I was pregnant. I remembered how I had danced for joy, thanking and praising God, when the second line appeared on my home pregnancy test, indicating that I was pregnant. Our first child was on its way. Life was good. God was good. And everything was right in the world.

As the first rays of dawn began to peek through the shutters of our bedroom window, I assured myself that everything was going to be all right. After all, God was in control, wasn't he?

Later that day I went about my business as if nothing had happened that morning. I had blood drawn for prenatal tests, stopped at the grocery store to purchase saltine crackers and milk, and come home again to rest.

Then it happened. The nightmare all over again. But now it was real. I started to bleed. Cold terror gripped me as I rushed to the doctor's office. This wasn't happening. It couldn't be happening.

As Rob and I sat in the waiting room, my mind felt numb, frozen with fear. I rocked back and forth in the chair, trying to think, trying not to think. Quietly Rob took my hand. His eyes met mine. But there were no words to say. My nightmare was coming true.

Within a few minutes we were ushered into a small examination room. The doctor, her usually cheerful face drawn with sympathy, pulled a cart of machinery up to the table. "We'll need to do an ultrasound, to see if—" She didn't finish her sentence. She didn't need to. I knew.

As she moved the probe at different angles, I saw nothing on the screen but gray fuzz. She shut off the machine. "I'm sorry. It's too late." The words were barely a whisper, yet they echoed through me like a shout: *It's too late. It's too late. It's too late.*

The baby was gone.

As we left the doctor's office, grief and shock mixed together, leaving me in a daze of pain. I prayed that I'd wake up again and find it wasn't true. I prayed that the doctor was somehow wrong, even though my own body confirmed the fact that I was no longer pregnant.

When we reached home, a dozen reminders of my loss assaulted me—a congratulations card on my desk, a baby name book on the coffee table, a bag of new maternity clothes sitting on the stairs waiting to be taken up to our bedroom.

I sat on the couch and stared at nothing. "Oh God," I whispered, and could get no further.

Slowly I reached for the baby name book and began flipping through the pages. My eyes lingered over the names we had marked: Andrew, Jared, Thomas . . . Brianna, Justine, Michelle. My heart lurched with each name.

"We never even knew if you were a boy or a girl," I whispered. "We'll never know now." Tears caught in my throat as I shut the book and tucked it under the couch. Soon I was putting the congratulations card and the maternity clothes under the couch, too. I felt Rob watching me, a look of real concern on his face. I picked up the journal that we had started for the baby and held it with trembling hands. My eyes, still wide with shock and pain, finally met Rob's.

"I know," he choked.

I fell to my knees, my head in my hands. "Oh God," I prayed. I remained there for some time, until in the midst of my grief and feeling of hopelessness, a single Scripture verse came to my mind. It wasn't one I would have expected. It wasn't one of comfort, or hope in God's power, or a promise of future blessing. Rather, it was a passage spoken by Job when he, too, was faced with tragedy: "The LORD gave and the LORD has taken away; may the name of the LORD be praised" (Job 1:21).

It was then that the tears came in a flood. I knew that God had given us a baby, and I was experiencing the agony of his taking the child away, but how could I praise him in the midst of a nightmare-come-true?

Still shaking, I rose and went into the other room to get Rob's guitar. As I came back to the living room, I handed it to him. "Play something for me," I whispered. "Not about me, about God."

Without a word, he took the guitar and began to play "Jesus Loves Me." The simple words washed through my mind, beckoning, questioning. Could I still sing them, even now?

Oh God, I can't. Help me, my mind cried. I squeezed my eyes shut, and with a shuddering breath I pushed the words past the lump in my throat: "Little ones to him belong. They are weak but he is strong. Yes, Jesus loves me. . . ."

I sang until, through my tears, I saw the cross. A comforting warmth filled me. *God understands the pain of losing a child*, I thought. *His Son died on the cross.* I drew a ragged breath. Was God allowing me to experience a bit of his own pain? If so, could I trust him to go through this nightmare with me and give me the strength to accept it without anger and accusation?

Another verse from Job came to me: "Shall we accept good from God, and not trouble?" (Job 2:10).

The words challenged me. If I praised God, if I claimed that God was good and just and kind when things were going well, then I needed to be able to say the same of him when things were not going well. If I only praised God when circumstances were good, what did that say about my faith?

I didn't want to be a "fair-weather" Christian. I wanted a faith that wasn't based on how happy my circumstances were, but on who God is. Circumstances change, but God stays the same. His glory and his love are constant, even in the worst of times. And this, I determined, was the very worst time of all. Worse even than all the negative pregnancy tests, worse than the months of hoping, only to be disappointed again, worse than the fear of never being able to get pregnant. One thing I knew. I couldn't get through this pain without him.

I began to sing, my voice wavering even as God comforted me, not with promises or platitudes, but with the awesome wonder of his presence. Minutes passed, and still I sang, in spite of the tears that still flowed unhindered down my cheeks. Even in the midst of a nightmare-come-true, I had to proclaim that God was good, loving, just, and holy. He was still worthy of my praise.

And yet as the months passed the sorrow surrounding the loss of our baby stayed with me like an ever-present weight in my heart. Doubts regarding God's love and questions about his care began to plague me again. "How could you take my baby from me, Lord?" I cried. "How could you love me and still put me through this pain?" But my prayers seemed to hit the ceiling and rain back down on me without answers.

As I struggled day after day, month after month, as friends looked at me, shook their heads, and asked, "Aren't you over it yet?" I again found Job to be my mentor. Job continued to call out to God, to turn to him with all his doubts, questions, and fears, despite the shallow answers offered by his friends and despite God's silence. Eventually God showed up for Job. So I, too, turned again and again to God, whether or not I felt like he was listening. And for me as well, God showed up, not in a storm, but in an increasing awareness of his presence coupled with a growing understanding of his character.

Finally I began to realize something that I'd never known before. God, it seemed, was less interested in my happiness than he was in the strength of my faith. Suffering and sorrow were not the enemies I had once thought, but were tools in the hands of a loving God, tools that could mold me into the woman God desired me to be. I only needed to keep seeking him, to keep pouring my pain and my doubts out to him.

Only then could he turn the misery of miscarriage into something worthwhile.

Now, years later, as I look back on my experience, I realize that I have been profoundly changed. Like Job, my understanding of God has grown. And though I still grieve the loss of our child, I know that God used that brief life for a purpose in his kingdom. I will never be the same. Because of that child, though lost so early, my faith no longer is based on the ever-changing circumstances of my life but on the unchanging glory and wonder of God. And now, through the window of deep suffering, I can see God more clearly.

TWELVE

I CAN'T TAKE THIS ANYMORE—THE PHYSICAL STRESS

Lynette, age 38

One more test. One more procedure. One more doctor poking around in places that I'd once thought were private. After countless blood tests to check my hormone levels; pap smears and pelvic exams; ultrasounds; months of basal body temperature charts and morning urine tests with the ovulation predictor kit; after having skinny tubes stuck in me for an endometrial biopsy and later for a hysterosalpingography; after postcoital tests and shots of Pergonal; how could I mind another procedure? But I did mind. I was sick of all the cold instruments, the instructions to "please strip from the waist down and wait here for the doctor," the charts, the pills, the shots, the bruises from taking blood. I was sick of counting the days and scraping together money for the next procedure. Of course, it didn't help that I hated needles, hated hospitals, hated tiny little examination rooms with not enough ventilation.

Yet here I stood on a cold tile floor with a skimpy hospital gown barely reaching my knees. My personal belongings were in a plastic sack beside me, and a fluorescent light flickered overhead. I curled my bare toes and shivered, aware that in a few minutes I would be wheeled down the hall to the operating room. Slowly I crawled into the bed, pulled up the thin sheet to cover my legs, and waited. I could hear my heart pounding in my ears.

Around me, a half dozen other patients lay in narrow beds awaiting their turn. The man next to me would be undergoing heart surgery, and the woman across the way was having a cancerous lump removed from her back—serious conditions, serious surgeries. Compared to them, I shouldn't have been worried. After all, I was only here for a laparoscopy, the last step in the diagnostic path of infertility. Four small incisions, a laser, and a scope—simple, the doctor said, but major surgery all the same. I trembled and wriggled my body lower on the bed.

A nurse sauntered over and flipped a blood pressure cuff around my upper arm. Pump, pump, pump, the band grew tighter, then slowly loosened. The nurse looked at me. "A little high," she murmured. "Not unusual before surgery. Do you want Valium?"

Another pill? Another drug? Wasn't surgery bad enough? "No, thanks," I muttered. Here I was, a healthy woman of thirty-something, going in for surgery because no one knew what was wrong. It seemed crazy. It felt crazy.

I shook my head. Treatment took so much time and too much energy. Somehow along the way I'd forgotten to do the things that made life fun. It had been months since I had gone for a bike ride or taken a walk in the woods. The flower box outside my kitchen window held only clumps of dirt. I used to plant purple and yellow pansies there every spring, but I hadn't done any planting for two years, not since Jack and I had started on the road of diagnosis and treatment. Why did infertility have to be so hard?

I clenched my fists and shut my eyes tight. I couldn't stand it anymore. How could I endure being poked or prodded one more time?

"Excuse me, ma'am."

My eyes flew open to see a nurse standing over me, needle in hand. I shuddered.

"We need to put the IV in now," she explained.

I tried to relax.

One jab. A miss. I turned my head. She'd try again. Ouch. There. The needle was in. I let out the breath I hadn't realized I was holding.

The nurse connected a clear tube to the needle. I glanced up to see a plastic bag filled with liquid hanging above me. I looked away.

The nurse bent over me. "Do you know what surgery you're having today?" she asked in a clipped tone.

"A laparoscopy," I answered.

She checked the chart. "And do you know what it's for?"

"Infertility." I said the word like a curse.

A look of sympathy softened her features. She smiled and patted me twice on the knee. "You'll be just fine. Don't worry," she said, then walked away.

Fine? Don't worry? I frowned and stared at the tube connected to my arm, then down at my toes poking from the bottom of the white hospital sheet. *I'm not doing this for nothing,* I reminded myself. If this helped me to get the baby I so wanted, then the pain and discomfort would be worth it. After all, my infertility wasn't only an emotional and spiritual crisis, it was a physical problem as well, a medical condition that might be treatable. And infertility treatment, just like the treatment for cancer, heart disease, or anything else, naturally came with doctors, needles, and uncomfortable exams. "Treatment is a good thing," I said aloud. But it didn't help. The question still remained: *How could I ease the stress of the physical part of my infertility? How could I make it bearable?* No matter the results of the laparoscopy, one thing I knew. I couldn't go on like this. Something had to change.

Three hours later the surgery was over. In the next few weeks, as I watched the incisions heal and made my way back to nearly normal, I thought about what I would do after I had recovered. During surgery the doctor had found patches of endometriosis, which he zapped away with a laser. He also removed cysts on my ovaries. He suggested I try intra-uterine insemination for three months, and if those failed, to go on to in vitro fertilization. In other words, more needles, more drugs, more trips to the hospital. But not yet. I needed to finish healing first. That meant there would be a couple of months with no temperature charts, no pills, and no procedures. A couple of months of "normal." I savored the thought.

And that's when it dawned on me. I had been doing too much, too quickly. With my biological clock ticking, I hadn't wanted to waste any time. But I wasn't Superwoman and I needed a break. Taking a month or a couple of months off here and there wasn't going to make that big of a difference in the whole scheme of things. And it just might keep me sane.

So as the time approached to continue treatment, I decided to do things differently from then on. Jack and I made a plan, deciding what procedures we would try and when we would do them, making sure to plan a few months off in between. And in those breaks, we did fun things like take a vacation to Yellowstone, plant a garden, and have a ceremony to renew our wedding vows. I also realized that if I was getting medical treatments, I should take care of myself. I should sleep and eat well, just like I'd do if I were being treated for any other medical problem.

Then in my everyday life I began to take time again for my normal outdoor activities, slowly at first, as I healed from surgery, but enough to enjoy a short bike ride, a walk in the park, or a kayaking trip down the American River. And, lo and behold, I eventually planted some pansies in the little box outside my kitchen window. They might not have meant much to someone else, but they were significant to me. I was getting my life back.

Later I discovered other small things to help ease the physical discom-fort of the procedures. During examinations, when the cold instruments poked and prodded me, I began to pray, not for myself, but for others. Prayer helped keep my mind focused on God and away from the uncomfortable procedure. Sometimes I'd pray for the child we hoped to have; that if God eventually did give us one, we would be wise parents; that we would know how to bring the child up with a knowledge of God. Other times I'd practice memorizing Scripture. My favorite was 2 Corinthians 12:9–10: "But he said to me, 'My grace is sufficient for you, for my power is made perfect in weakness.' Therefore I will boast all the more gladly about my weaknesses, so that Christ's power may rest on me. That is why, for Christ's sake, I delight in weaknesses, in insults, in hardships, in persecutions, in difficulties. For when I am weak, then I am strong."

Of course, I still disliked doctor appointments. They continued to be difficult. But turning to God, knowing what was coming, and looking forward to fun times away from it all helped me to endure treatment longer, long enough for it to work. And, after our second IVF cycle, we finally conceived.

After seven years, we had our first child, a little girl we named Sarah Marie. And I must say, after all the infertility treatments, the shots, and the hospital visits, I wasn't afraid of labor and delivery. It was hard, and it hurt like crazy, but I was used to pain and discomfort. God prepared me for it. He made me tough in those years when I battled infertility; but more importantly, through the maze of tests and treatments, God taught me that sometimes it's good to slow down and plant a few pansies.

THIRTEEN

DECISIONS, DECISIONS—HOW FAR SHOULD WE GO?

Brooke and Dan, ages 40 and 41

I never dreamed I'd have trouble conceiving a second time. I had a child out of wedlock when I was twenty, so now that I was thirty-two, married, and ready for more children, I assumed I'd get pregnant right away. No problem, right? After all, I hadn't even been trying the first time. But sometimes life doesn't turn out the way we think it will.

After two years without a pregnancy, Dan and I went through the usual tests, then tried fertility drugs, all to no avail. Our insurance didn't cover infertility treatments, so the money soon ran low.

"Have you tried insemination? What about that test tube thing?" my friends would ask. And invariably they would tell me about how this or that procedure worked for some distant relative or acquaintance.

"Oh no, we haven't tried that yet," I'd answer politely, all the while thinking, *Do you know how much that costs?!* There was no way we could afford anything like in vitro fertilization. Even an insemination was more than our budget could bear.

Besides, I had a lot of ethical questions regarding IVF. If we ever got the money, I knew I wouldn't want to do selective reduction. And I wasn't sure what I thought about the idea of freezing extra embryos. How much would I really be willing to do to "help nature along"?

I didn't think I'd ever have to decide, until one day Dan came home from work, threw his jacket across the couch, and announced, "Guess what? I'm getting a bonus. What do you want to do with the money?"

Possibilities flew through my mind. "How much?" I whispered.

"Not quite enough for IVF, but we could try to borrow the rest, if you want. Or we could do a few inseminations and have a little extra money to put away."

When Dan received his bonus a week later, we thought and prayed about what we should do and finally settled on the inseminations. IVF was just too much money to risk on a procedure that might not work.

But three inseminations and a couple of thousand dollars later, we were still no better off than before. And so the end came, just like that.

The decision for us was a practical one. We didn't want to get a loan that we'd never be able to repay. Instead, we used the money we had. When it was gone, we stopped treatment. It was as simple as that.

Today I wonder if the result would have been different if we'd had all the money in the world. But somehow I think it would have ended up the same. Still, I've decided I can't play the game of "what if" and "maybe." Sometimes you just have to do your best to make a good decision, and then be content with the results. Even when things don't turn out the way you'd hoped.

Valerie and Doug, ages 36 and 40

In our society it's not popular to quit. I grew up knowing that quitters were to be scorned. It's those who persevere, those who press on, who win the prize. So, when it came to my infertility, I applied the same principle. If I just kept going and didn't give up, then I was sure to get the baby I wanted so badly. So press on I did, dragging my husband with me, through tests and treatments, multiple months on Clomid, then Fertinex, followed by IUI, IVF, ICSI, and ZIFT. But nothing worked.

Eventually our savings were drained and our credit cards maxed out. I knew my doctor better than I knew my husband, and I still wasn't pregnant. But I couldn't quit. After all, the next procedure could be the one.

It took a visit from my mother to bring me to my senses.

"I'm thinking of trying GIFT next," I told her over a cup of coffee.

My mother opened a packet of Sweet 'N Low, sprinkled it into her cup, and stirred. "What does Doug think of that?"

I snorted. "He doesn't understand. He thinks it's too expensive."

"Is it?" she asked without looking up.

"It's thirteen thousand dollars. No more than the two IVF procedures we tried. This time, I'm thinking of borrowing the money against the house." I stared into my coffee cup. "I guess Doug is worried about not being able to pay back the loan afterward." I took a sip of my coffee. "I just can't comprehend how he can think of quitting before we've exhausted every option."

Mom placed her spoon carefully on a napkin, then looked up at me. "Exhausted. That's a good choice of words." She paused, as if waiting for me to respond. When I didn't, she continued. "Val, honey, have you ever considered that Doug might simply be tired of all the disappointments and debts?"

I drew up my shoulders. "Are you saying we should quit?"

"Hmmm." Mom adjusted her glasses, swirled the coffee in her cup, and took a small sip before she answered. "What did you say was the name of the procedure you're considering now?"

I crossed my arms. "It's called GIFT."

"GIFT. How appropriate," she whispered.

I frowned. "What do you mean?"

Mom tapped her fingers three times on the counter, and that's when I knew she was about to speak her mind, no holds barred. She cleared her throat. "Valerie, don't you think it's about time you realized that a child is a gift from God? It's not something you earn by perseverance and hard work. God is ultimately the one who gives children."

I opened my mouth to speak, but Mom cut me off. "Now, I'm not saying there's anything wrong with pursuing treatment, but what I am saying is that you need to talk to God about it. Ask him if it's time for you to move on with your life." Her voice softened. "You know I want grandchildren more than anything, but not at the expense of your marriage or your health or your sanity."

I shook my head. "I'm not a quitter. Dad always said so."

Mom got up and came over to give me a hug. "Don't think of it as quitting, sweetheart, but as moving on. You and Doug, together with God, should decide if it's time. Promise me you'll at least pray about it."

I stood and squeezed Mom closer. "I promise," I whispered in her ear.

The following day Doug and I sat down together on the couch and asked God to guide us. As we sat there in the presence of God, I began to feel something that I hadn't felt in a very long time. I began to feel a sense of peace, of closure.

Infertility had been consuming our lives, draining Doug and me not only financially but also emotionally. I was weary. Doug was weary. Perhaps we really had tried long enough.

Doug stood and retrieved a notebook and pencil from a drawer in the kitchen. I watched him write one thing after another, listing everything we had done to try to have a baby—all the tests, all the procedures, all the medications. As I stared at the list, I understood, at last, that one more procedure wasn't going to make a difference. We had done everything we could. And now it was over. It was time to say, "Enough."

Sometimes I still wonder if we gave up too soon. *What if we had tried it just one more time?* I ask myself. But then I look back and remember the stress and the frustration, and I remind myself that we made the right decision. Like Mom said, it was time to end the journey and move on with our lives.

Carlos and Kim, ages 45 and 37

Kim and I knew when we married that having children was going to be a challenge. I had two kids from a previous marriage and had undergone a vasectomy after the second one was born. Now I regretted that decision, just as I regretted so many things from my past, before I became a Christian. Still, regrets wouldn't produce the children that Kim and I hoped to have. I thought a simple surgery to reverse the vasectomy would do the trick, but it didn't. And that's when we knew that we would be travelers on the bumpy road of infertility.

Kim had a friend who had also traveled this difficult road, and she told us, "Infertility isn't a state, it's a journey—a painful and sometimes long journey through places you never thought you'd have to go."

Well, I thought, *if infertility is a journey, we have to know where it will go, and more importantly, when it will end.* We needed a plan of action.

So after our initial trip to the infertility clinic, Kim and I sat down at our kitchen table and spread out all the information from the clinic in piles around us. Slowly we read through the pamphlets and papers until we understood what we'd be facing, at least medically. Then we took a pad of paper and began to write out our plan based on how much we thought we could endure, the odds of success, and the state of our finances. Having a plan, I knew, would help us to bring reason and wisdom to a decision fraught with emotion.

At our next appointment, we shared our plan with the doctor and did some rearranging and fine-tuning. Then we took the sheet and put it in our "important stuff" drawer. Every time we completed one step on the chart, we'd cross it off. I must admit, having the list didn't ease the pain of infertility, but at least it helped us to see how far we had come and to know that this journey wouldn't go on forever. Indeed, the end came six years after we'd begun. I'll never forget that day when we crossed off the last item.

I held the pen over the paper while Kim stood beside me. "This is it," I whispered. "It's over."

She nodded. I could see the tears forming in the corners of her eyes. "I never really thought it would come to this," she said quietly. "I thought we'd be pregnant before we got halfway through the plan."

"I know." I took her hand in mine and, with the other, crossed out the final line.

Together we took the paper, crumpled it, and threw it into the fireplace. Then we lit the fire and stood before the flames.

"I didn't think this would hurt so much," she said.

I glanced at her. The firelight flickered off her hair, bringing out the auburn highlights. She was beautiful. I loved her. And I would have given her a child if I could have. But now there was nothing I could do but watch the paper burn.

"I'm sorry," I mumbled.

She smiled, a sad, understanding smile that shot to my heart. "It's good to know where the end is. I couldn't have gone on like that month after month, year after year."

I nodded. "We'll be okay."

She put her arm around me. "I know we will. Eventually."

The paper withered in the flame and turned to gray ash. Then we turned from the fireplace, walked away, and didn't look back.

FOURTEEN

AM I LESS OF A WOMAN?

Kelli, age 36

I knew what it meant to be a woman. I'd always known. It meant being a "mommy." At least that's what I'd always believed.

Even now a doll sits high on the shelves in my bedroom. Her dark curly hair is mussed and worn. The pink ribbon that once adorned her hair was lost long ago. Her blue dress is torn, and she's missing one shoe. But I love that doll, because she embodies the hopes and dreams of my childhood. With her I played house and had tea parties. I sang her to sleep at night. I practiced for the child I knew I would someday have when I was all grown up.

So imagine my surprise when I discovered that my girlhood dreams might never become a reality. My husband and I married in our early twenties and planned to start a family soon after we'd said our "I do's." But the years went by, and still I didn't get pregnant. Everyone said we were young yet, to give it time. But time didn't give us the child we longed for, even after trips to the infertility clinic and treatments I was sure would work. And still, as the years passed, the doll sat on the shelf, looking down at me, reminding me of the baby I'd always dreamed of and still didn't have.

Everywhere around me children played. In the nursery at church, at the park down the road, in the street in front of my house. And for each laugh I heard, for every shout of *"Mom-myyy,"* my feelings of emptiness grew. How could I ever live a full life without children? How could I be a fulfilled woman if I was never a mom?

These feelings haunted me and culminated at a community Easter egg hunt held at our church. I sat at the beverage table, pouring punch into tiny paper cups as children dressed in their Easter finery scampered around the lawn hunting for plastic eggs. "Mommy, look!" called a little girl who looked surprisingly like my childhood doll, rumpled brown hair and all. She held up her basketful of eggs and grinned. "I got sixteen eggs!"

Her mother smiled. "That's great, Ashleigh," she said, then turned back to the group of women gathered around the welcome center.

I grimaced and began to mix up another batch of punch as the world of women with children swirled around me. A girl and her mom, dressed in matching flowered skirts, fancy hats, and white gloves, skipped hand in hand down the walkway toward the church. One mother near the door stooped over to straighten the tie of her toddler son. A younger woman casually breastfed her baby next to the face-painting booth, while another showed off the new baby she'd had only two weeks before. And, as if that wasn't bad enough, a few moments later a group of women paused in front of the punch table as they chatted about their pregnancies.

"I was in labor for twenty-six hours," said one.

"That's nothing, my sister went forty before having a C-section," added a woman in yellow.

"I thought I was going to die!" claimed another. "But when I saw little Jeremiah's face for the first time, I forgot about all the pain."

A woman in her fifties chuckled and turned to a younger woman, who was rubbing her rounded belly. "Honey, go with the epidural. You won't feel a thing."

The pregnant woman twisted a lock of blond hair between her fingers. "Does it really hurt that much?"

A dreamy look crossed the older woman's face. "It's worth every minute. The birth of my son was the most beautiful moment of my life. Holding him in my arms for the first time—" her voice trailed off. Then she sighed. "You haven't really lived until you've given birth," she added.

The others nodded in agreement.

The pregnant woman smiled. "You know," she said, "this pregnancy has been a pretty incredible experience in itself, feeling the baby kick and squirm, watching my tummy quiver when she gets the hiccups." Her smile broadened as she gave her belly a quick pat. "I never really knew the full meaning of womanhood until I started to feel this little life growing inside me."

I felt my heart constrict as I listened. All the hurt and disappointment of infertility rose within me until I thought I would drown beneath the onslaught. Couldn't these women tell that their words were like swords in my heart? Didn't they know that I might never experience the feeling of having a child grow inside me? Never know the joy of watching my abdomen stretch with the promise of a new life? How could that woman stand there patting her belly so blissfully while I died a little more every minute? Tears gathered in my eyes. Desperately I fought them back.

The conversation continued as one of the women smiled at me and then leaned over to pick up a cup of punch. "Becky's due in May," she said to me. "Any words of advice for her?"

I swallowed hard and shook my head. "I-I don't have any children," I said, almost choking on the words.

Her look held a strange combination of pity and disapproval. "Oh, that's too bad." She turned back to the group. "Let's stand over there in the sun. Oh, look!" She gestured toward the lawn. "Brianna's found one of the prize eggs. She takes after her Daddy, I guess—"

I watched them go. The tears I'd been holding at bay soon began to slip down my cheeks. I set down the pitcher and hurried into the empty church, where I hoped to be safe from both sympathetic glances and words that pierced my heart with pain.

The tears came faster as I entered the sanctuary. Surrounding the altar, dozens of Easter lilies bent their snowy heads toward the long rows of wooden pews. Behind them, an empty cross hung against the front wall. And above, three stained-glass windows captured any sunlight that peeked through the overcast sky. Through a blur of tears, I looked at the third window. There, Christ stood in the clouds, his arms extended toward me, his palms bright red where a shard of blood-colored glass marked the place where the nails had driven deep.

I sat in the first pew and glanced from the window to the cross to the painting of an empty tomb that hung along the side of the altar area. Everywhere I saw the symbols of resurrection, of new life and hope. So why did I feel so hopeless, so empty?

My gaze fell to a place at the altar, a particular place, a special spot.

There, a dozen years before, I had knelt and given my life to Christ. I remembered how He filled my heart and promised to live there. I remembered how happy I had felt, how full of life. But that was then. Now after years of struggling through the doubts and disappointments of infertility, things seemed different.

I rose from the first pew and walked toward the altar. Slowly I knelt again in the same place I had twelve years before. I tilted my head until I could see the third stained-glass window above me. "Right here, Lord," I whispered. "Here's where you promised me that you'd never leave me or forsake me. And here's where I surrendered my life to you."

As I said the words, light began to shine through the stained-glass window above me. One ray shone through the blood-colored shard on Jesus' palm and sent a shaft of red light shooting across the altar in front of me. My gaze returned to the window and I saw again the image of Jesus, his eyes gentle, his arms extended. "You are not your own," I heard the words whisper through my mind. "You were bought with a price."

And that's when I realized the truth. I did have a life growing within me. Christ's life. He lived in me. I was not empty, not barren, after all.

I stayed at the altar a few more minutes. Long enough to tell him that I'd really meant it when I surrendered my life to him all those years ago. I asked him again to fill my heart, to take my life and make it his, to help me to see beyond my hurt and to accept the path he chose for me.

As light continued to pour down from the window above, I finally began to understand that giving my life to Christ meant that he could do what he wanted with it. And whatever life he chose, whether it included children or not, would be a good life, a fulfilled life.

Years have passed since that Easter morning when the light shone through the third window and into my heart, and still my doll sits on the shelf at home waiting to see if there will ever be another little girl to play with her.

My desire for a baby remains strong. I still hope and pray that some-day my childhood dreams will become reality. But for now, I know I must accept the idea that my belly may never grow round with child, I may never feel the kicks of tiny feet within me. But even if no one ever calls me "Mommy," I remember that my life is not my own, but Christ's who lives in me. So I will trust God to make my life worthwhile. I can still be all he wants me to be. I can still live a fulfilled life in him.

I know that whether or not I ever have children, I am still fully a woman, and more importantly, I am a woman of God.

FIFTEEN

AM I LESS OF A MAN?

Greg, age 30

I thought my self-image was unshakable. I thought I could handle anything. After all, I was a man's man. A tackle-football, monster-truck, built-Ford-tough type of guy. But then the test results came in.

The phone rang, and I answered it with my usual "Hey, this is Greg."

The nurse from our infertility clinic was on the other end of the line. "Hello, Mr. Smith, this is Jean," she said. "I have the test results for you and your wife."

"Oh, uh, okay." I swallowed. "What's the scoop?"

"Everything looks fine for Claire, but your numbers are, well"—she paused—"quite low."

I felt my stomach twist. "Low? What do you mean by low?"

"Your sperm count came in at three million per milliliter. Normal is between twenty and one hundred and fifty million."

Three? Only three million? "But, but," I sputtered. "Are you sure? Maybe there's been a mistake."

"We're very careful with these tests, Mr. Smith."

"Still . . ."

"Have you been sick with a high fever in the last few months? Or perhaps you've been in a hot tub."

"Uh, no." My grip tightened on the receiver. Slowly I lowered myself to the chair near the phone. "So"—my voice wavered—"what do we do now?"

"Well, we can test you again in a couple of weeks, if you'd like. Other than that, the doctor will be happy to discuss options at your next appointment. You're coming in with Claire on Monday, aren't you?"

"Sure, I guess so." I barely muttered the words. *Three million. Only three.* The number pounded through my head. I was okay when I thought it was something with my wife that was keeping us from having children. But this, this was different. I was the one with the problem. It was my sperm that were lacking, my fault we weren't able to conceive.

I hung up the phone quietly.

"Who was that, honey?" my wife called from the other room.

"The clinic."

"What did they want?" Claire walked into the room and tossed the towel she was folding onto the kitchen counter.

For a moment I didn't answer.

She looked at me and raised one eyebrow, just like she always does when she thinks I'm acting strangely.

I rubbed my hand over the counter top and glanced away. "The test results are in."

"And?"

"Low sperm count," I mumbled, too quietly for her to hear.

"What?"

"Low sperm count," I said again, just a little louder.

"Oh. Did they say anything about my tests?"

"Yours are all okay."

"So now we know what the problem is." Her eyes caught and held mine. "Do you want to talk about it?"

Absolutely not, I thought. But I only shook my head, turned, and went into the garage. "Got some work to do," I called behind me. "I'm going to Sam's Hardware." A trip to Sam's was just what I needed to gather my thoughts. If I could hold a few wrenches, try out a couple of power tools, I'd feel fine again.

So I took my trip to the hardware store. I strolled around the tool aisles. I even bought a new table saw. And slowly the implications of those disturbing test results receded to the back of my mind—until Claire and I attended a party at a friend's house a few weeks later.

We were casually chatting with friends. Claire was on the couch with a group of women and I was standing by the TV when I overheard what she was saying.

"Greg's got a low sperm count," I heard her say.

Maybe it was my imagination, but the room seemed to fall silent. Quickly I looked around, hoping the other guys hadn't heard. But my best friend, Jerry, patted me on the shoulder and gave me a sympathetic look. "Hey, that's too bad, man. Sorry to hear it."

"What's up?" Adam walked over with a Pepsi in his hand.

Jerry turned to him. "Greg's got a low sperm count."

I felt myself shrinking.

Adam took a swig of his soda and made some remark that I'd rather not repeat.

I tried to fake a chuckle, but it seemed to get stuck behind my tonsils and came out like a choking cough. I cleared my throat and turned toward Jerry, hoping to change the subject before it got any worse. "So how's the job going?" I asked. "Heard you were up for a promotion."

Jerry dropped his hand from my shoulder. He seemed nervous. "Job's going great. I'm looking at getting that raise and promotion any day now."

"Bet Margaret's glad to hear that."

"Yeah, she's pretty excited about having a few extra dollars every month."

The conversation stayed on Jerry's job for a few more minutes before we turned to everyone's picks for the upcoming Super Bowl. I breathed a sigh of relief. Football was a safe topic. Talking about quarterbacks and pass plays kept the conversation from turning back to more personal issues. Still, for the rest of the evening, I pasted on my fake smile while becoming more and more angry with Claire for sharing our private information.

On the way home from the party, my anger boiled over. "What were you thinking, Claire?" I said through gritted teeth.

My wife glanced at me with a confused look on her face. "What are you talking about?"

I tapped my fingers on the steering wheel and glared at her before turning my eyes back to the road. "Oh, come on, you know what I mean. Telling everybody about my sperm count! Don't you think that is a little private?"

"What's the big deal? Ann asked me if we'd found out what was wrong, and I told her."

"You didn't need to mention my low sperm count." I couldn't believe she didn't think it was a big deal.

From the corner of my eye, I saw Claire looked somewhat amused. "If we'd found out I had problems with my ovaries or had a blocked fallopian tube, you wouldn't have any objection to my telling Ann about that."

"That's different."

"What is different about it?"

I slammed my hand against the steering wheel. "Look, my sperm count is private. I don't want you telling anyone about it. No one. *Especially* our friends."

"Okay, then, what am I supposed to say when someone asks? Lie?"

"I don't know. I don't care. Just don't talk about my sperm count!"

Claire shook her head and turned toward the side window. "All right, all right, I didn't know you were so sensitive about it."

I stared out into the rainy night. The only sound was the sloshing of the windshield wipers. I didn't really know why I'd reacted so severely. Of course, I was a little embarrassed. But Claire was right. If it had been her problem, I wouldn't have thought twice about telling friends the test results. But I felt differently about it when it was *my* problem. How could she not understand that? How could she not understand that a low sperm count was something that hit a man hard, something you just didn't share in a group?

Now that the sperm issue was out there, I did what I figured any real man would do—I ignored it. Oh, I swallowed a few extra vitamins, took cooler showers, and stayed away from the hot tub, but other than that I simply refused to think about it. But my friend Jerry changed my mind.

I hadn't seen him since the party, so I thought I'd stop by and surprise him at work. But I was the one in for a surprise.

I opened the glass door and stepped up to the receptionist's desk. "Hi, I'm here to see Jerry."

The woman glanced up at me and frowned. "Jerry doesn't work here anymore."

I stepped back. "What? Of course he does."

She shook her head. "Jerry was laid off two months ago."

Two months ago? That would be a month before the party. Surely if Jerry had lost his job he would have told me. Something strange was going on, and I needed to find out what it was. I mumbled "thanks" to the receptionist and hurried out to my car.

I finally tracked Jerry down that night in his garage. He was lying beneath the chassis of his 1967 Mustang. "Hey, Jerry!" I called.

He slid out from under the car. "Greg! Good to see you, man. I didn't hear you come in. What's up?"

I crossed my arms. "I don't know, buddy. Why don't you tell me?"

Jerry wiped his hands on his overalls, then stood up. "What do you mean?"

"I stopped by your work today."

An awkward silence fell between us. Jerry turned away to finish cleaning his hands on a rag. He refused to look at me. "Guess you know then."

"They told me you were laid off two months ago."

"Yeah."

"So what was all that talk at the party about a promotion?"

He shrugged and turned back to me. "I just couldn't bring myself to tell you guys that I didn't have a job."

"Does Margaret know?"

Jerry twisted the rag in his hand. "No."

"*No?*"

"I leave every morning and come back in the evening, same as I've always done. Only instead of going to a job, I'm looking for one."

"You're kidding me."

"I wish I were."

He looked like a dejected puppy. I draped an arm around his shoulders. "Gosh, man, you should have told me. I could have tried to help, or at least prayed for you."

"What? And have you guys think I'm a loser? No thanks."

"Come on, Jerry. You are not a loser because you've lost your job. Our self-worth is found in God, anyway, not in our job. You know that as well as I do."

"Yeah, I guess I do."

"Hey, I hope you find something real soon. And remember to let your friends know the next time something important happens in your life, huh?"

Jerry's eyes locked with mine. "Yeah, like you told us about your sperm count being low."

"Well, that's different," I mumbled.

"Yeah, right."

We stood there for a moment without speaking. "Look, I gotta go. I'll stop by tomorrow and see how the job hunt's coming."

As I drove away, Jerry's words haunted me. I had to admit the truth. The low sperm count made me feel less of a man, just like his job loss made him feel. And while those reactions may be perfectly natural, they showed how we were finding at least part of our identity in something besides our relationship with Christ.

For the next several months I considered what it meant to be a man in God's sight. I thought about how Jesus proved himself through obedience to God. I also thought about the great price that Christ paid for me on the cross. I thought about how a man should be measured by the greatness of his faith, not by his sperm count. But it wasn't until I stumbled on the words of Isaiah 56:3–5 that I really began to understand that my identity doesn't come from my ability to procreate, but from the God who made me the man that I am: "Let not any eunuch complain, 'I am only a dry tree.' For this is what the LORD says: 'To the eunuchs who keep my Sabbaths, who choose what pleases me and hold fast to my covenant—to them I will give within my temple and its walls a memorial and a name better than sons and daughters; I will give them an everlasting name that will not be cut off' " (Isaiah 56:3–5).

If God didn't think less of me because I had fewer sperm than other guys, what right did I have to think less of myself?

These days I find that I'm much more at peace with my condition. While I still don't want my wife talking about my sperm count at parties, I find that I can accept the fact that our fertility problems lie with me. It's God who makes me who I am, and by his grace I am content with that—no matter what the numbers read.

STRUGGLES OF THE SPIRIT

Sixteen

If God Really Loved Me . . .

Patty, age 39

"Jesus loves me, this I know, for the Bible tells me so. . . ." It's such a simple song. I learned it as a child and sang it probably a thousand times. I never thought to doubt it until a few short years ago. After all, God's love was the first thing I learned about in Sunday school; it's the most basic element of faith, a truth that even the newest Christian believes. So why did I, a believer for twenty years, suddenly have my doubts?

It was my thirty-fifth birthday. Thirty-five is a milestone of sorts, when all the good statistics for pregnancy decrease, while the bad ones take a giant leap forward. Of course, I'd always planned to have a houseful of children by the time I was thirty-five, so the stats weren't going to matter. But my plans obviously weren't the same as God's.

So here I was turning thirty-five with no more to show for the years than withering hopes and dying dreams.

I would have liked to spend the day huddled in a corner with my tears, but my husband, Ted, planned a small party for me instead. It was an intimate affair—just a few close friends. Ted had worked hard to make everything perfect. Balloons were attached to the banister, and a cake with candles sat on the table next to the party hats and whistles. It all looked so cheerful, so bright, so it-doesn't-matter-that-I'm-thirty-five-and-still-don't-have-children. The least I could do was pretend to have a good time.

Soon our friends arrived, their faces all smiles, their arms full of gifts. Ted opened the door, and I greeted them with what I hoped was a believable smile.

"Happy birthday, old lady," Wayne grinned as he stepped through the doorway and deposited a package on the end table. After him came Sue, Lisa, Sam, and finally my best friend, Lynn.

"How are you doing?" Lynn whispered as she gave me a hug. "I've been thinking about you all day."

"I'm, uh, okay," I murmured back. "What's one more year?" I willed my voice to remain steady.

"Hmmm," she answered, then smiled gently and looked around. "Well, at least Ted didn't get those awful black balloons and streamers. He gets two points for sensitivity. But only two." With that cryptic comment, she tossed her sweater onto the arm of the couch and walked over to inspect the cake.

The rest of the party was uneventful. I made my wish—not to spit all over the cake—and blew out the candles. I groaned appropriately when I opened the few gag gifts from the others—the little-old-lady cane from Sue and Wayne, the bottle of Geritol from Lisa, the extra-large-print Bible from Lynn and Sam. I made a few remarks and cut an especially big piece of chocolate cake for Wayne, since he'd been caught sneaking a piece early at the last party we'd been to. I smiled at all the right times and laughed when I was supposed to. On the outside, I appeared to be holding together. But inside, I felt my heart breaking a little more every minute with the nagging thought that my hopes for a child would most likely never become reality.

As the evening drew to a close, I gathered up the cake plates and took them into the kitchen. *Why did this day have to be like this? I am no further away from conception than I was yesterday or will be tomorrow. But turning thirty-five is harder than I expected it to be.*

"Hey, are you okay? What's up?"

I turned to see Lynn, her hands full of cups and napkins.

"I'm *thirty-five*," I answered, as if that should explain everything.

Lynn looked at me for a moment. "It's the baby thing, isn't it?" Her voice was gentle. "I thought today might be hard for you, but you seemed to be doing so well."

"Appearances can be deceiving," I sighed. "You know, this all started eight years ago. It seems more like an eternity." I shook my head. "I remember when Ted finally got the promotion we'd been waiting for, and we had a little money saved." I grabbed a crumpled napkin and threw it toward the garbage can. "Everything was all set for kids—or so we thought."

Lynn picked up the napkin that had missed the trash and began rinsing the dishes. "Infertility can be a real surprise," she said at last. "I really thought you'd get pregnant right away. I can't believe it's taken so long."

"Why *has* it taken so long? Does God hate me or something?" I tried to hold the frustration from my voice. "What does God have against me anyway?"

Lynn didn't answer.

A cynical laugh escaped my lips as I opened the door to the dishwasher. "Ted and I were so naïve. We kept thinking God would surely bless us. 'Any month now,' we'd say, believing that we'd soon be rejoicing and thanking God, and all the doubts and pain would be behind us. 'God's timing is perfect,' we told each other. I remember telling Ted, 'God is just waiting for you to get settled in your new job. Or maybe he wants me to finish up with the teen Bible study I'm leading. Then I'll have plenty of time to rest and get ready for the baby.' What a joke!" I lined up the plates on the rack. "I was so sure we'd be standing up in church and testifying about God's faithfulness to us." I dropped the forks into the silverware bin and continued my ranting. "But Ted's been in that new job for eight years, and I haven't taught the teens in ages. So why don't I get pregnant? Where's my assurance that God loves me?"

Lynn sighed. "I don't know, Patty. I wish I did. It's too bad that last IUI didn't work. I really thought this might be the month. I'm so sorry."

"So am I. I just don't understand why God won't bless us with children. I read my Bible, I pray diligently, and I've claimed all the promises about answered prayer that I can find in the Scriptures. But nothing works." I paused while Lynn retrieved the rest of the cups from the other room. When she returned, I continued. "God can't say no forever, can he? After all, the psalms say to 'delight yourself in the Lord, and He will give you the desires of your heart.' And I desire a baby of my own more than anything else. It's okay if God doesn't choose to give me other blessings. He doesn't need to give me a fancy home, a new car, fame or fortune. I just want a baby! Is that too much to ask?"

Again, Lynn didn't answer me.

"Well, is it?"

Lynn frowned. "I wish I had some answers for you, Patty, but I don't. I know you've been faithful. I know you've delighted yourself in him. I know you try to do what God wants, not to earn a baby, but just because you love him and want to please him. So why you're still childless is a mystery to me."

I thought about all the grievances I had against God. It felt good, I decided, to finally voice the doubts and fears that had been haunting me for so long.

"Maybe all that stuff about God loving us is really just a bunch of garbage," I said dejectedly.

"You know that's not true."

"Do I? God knows how much I want a baby. His not giving me one seems more like cruelty than love. If my husband had the ability to give me a child but refused to, we'd call it abuse."

Lynn's tone remained calm: "Calling God cruel is a strong accusation."

I took a deep breath, attempting to compose myself. "Cruelty is being disposed to inflict pain or suffering. I looked it up in Webster's the other day." I choked over the words, tears welling in my eyes. "I don't understand why God doesn't love me."

Lynn gently put her arms around me and drew me close. "I know it's hard. Doubts are normal when you've been through as much as you have. But one thing I know, God does loves you. And I love you, too."

Lynn held me until her words settled in my heart. I was not alone.

I remembered all the times she had gone down to the altar with me, prayed for me, wept with me. I remembered when she waited with me for the results of my fifth home pregnancy test. She'd cried harder than I did that time, even though she had four healthy children at home. She drove me to the hospital for my HSG test and took me for ice cream afterward to celebrate finding only one tube blocked. Whatever else I doubted, one thing I knew: Lynn cared about me. Of course, others did, too. My friends from church, my family, my co-workers. But Lynn's concern showed me God's love in a tangible way, in a way I couldn't disregard. She made God real to me there in my own kitchen, when my doubts raged hotter than thirty-five birthday candles and my heart was heavy with grief. When my faith was weakest, she helped me to believe in God's love again, because it was there in front of me, lived out in a real person. I saw Jesus in Lynn, in Lisa, and Sue. I was reminded of his love for me on the cross, love enough to bear the pain, to suffer for me.

Over the next several weeks I thought about Christ's sacrifice for me. I didn't rush past his death to the joy of his resurrection, like I'd always done in the past. Before, I never wanted to contemplate the cross, only the empty tomb. I didn't want to see the sorrow, only the joy. It was the same, I realized, with my infertility. I never wanted to truly face it. Instead, I always tried to rush ahead to the prospect of having a baby. I thought that if I just believed strongly enough, I'd never have to face the hurt, the loss.

But God forced me to pause and consider the cost of the cross. The cross meant pain, shame, and suffering. The empty tomb meant joy and fulfillment. But one doesn't come without the other. Suffering, I discovered, is a part of life. Sorrow is a partner on the path to Christlikeness. God's priority is our relationship with him—knowing him, his sorrow and suffering as well as his joy. And if that was the case, I could no longer use my happiness as a measure of God's love.

In the four years since my thirty-fifth birthday, I've come to accept the idea that sometimes things just don't make sense. The cross didn't make sense to those who watched Jesus die. It was a strange demonstration of love. But in hindsight, we understand the sacrifice, the love that held Christ on the cross.

So perhaps someday I'll look back on these painful years of infertility and see there, as well, the marks of God's love for me. For now, I can only look to the cross and remember that he, too, knows what it means to hurt. I can only look into the eyes of those in whom he lives and see that he loves me. No matter how much sorrow I might feel.

When hope lies in tattered ruins
And faith is on its knees,
God's love embraces me
Until my darkness flees.

SEVENTEEN

IT'S NOT FAIR!

James, age 34

I looked out into the congregation and tried to figure out what would get these people to worship. "Oh God," I prayed, "please send your Holy Spirit. If only they could sense your presence. Just once!" It seemed that I had preached a thousand sermons about the greatness of God. Yet there they sat, vacantly staring at their hymnals, barely mouthing one of the most awesome songs ever written: "Then sings my soul, my Savior God to Thee. How great Thou art! How great Thou art!" How could anyone mumble those words? I closed my eyes and hoped that I, at least, could experience the awesome presence of God. Then it happened.

"Eeeee, don't touch me! Aaahh! Noooo!" Two youngsters came screaming out of the nursery, flew down the center aisle, and bounded across the front row of pews. I groaned. It wasn't as if this hadn't happened before. In fact, it was a weekly occurrence. Only the faces of the children changed. Which two of the Henderson kids was it this time? Members of the congregation, barely able to stay focused on their pathetic singing, were again distracted. The looks on their faces said it all. Anger, annoyance, confusion. All at once, dozens of eyes turned to Deb

Henderson, who was seated near the back row. Oblivious to the distraction, she nursed the newest member of her family while trying to control her two-year-old with her right arm.

Deb was practically a single mom. At least her husband never seemed to be around. So my wife and I were trying to minister to her and counsel her through some difficult times, most of which were associated with the fact that she had six children and very little means to provide for them. Keeping them under control in church was the least of her problems.

Just as the two toddlers circled the second pew on my right, a large hand reached out and nabbed both of them by the arms. The next thing I knew, Mr. Elsworth was firmly escorting the children to the back of the sanctuary. Their little feet barely touched the ground as they squealed and shouted all the way. This was the first time a member of the congregation had taken such drastic action. I hoped Deb wouldn't be offended.

"Pastor. PASTOR!" my music director hissed. I jumped to my feet and strode to the pulpit to begin the congregational prayer. Maybe there wouldn't be any further interruptions.

After the service, I greeted people at the front door, and noticed Deb Henderson, children in tow, drawing closer and closer. Anticipating conflict, I greeted her with the biggest smile I could muster. But instead of saying what I expected her to say, she looked up at me with a curious expression on her face. "Guess what, Pastor Jim. I'm pregnant! Isn't it wonderful?"

I cannot explain the flood of emotions I experienced at that moment. But I can tell you that the word *wonderful* wouldn't have described any of them. Awful thoughts raced through my mind. *Pregnant? Again? You've got to be kidding! You can't take care of the children you have now.* I tried hard to congratulate her while maintaining the huge fake smile, but I must have failed.

"Oh my," she said, as if reading my thoughts. "I'm sorry. I know you and Susan have been trying to have a baby."

It was one of the most awkward moments of my ministry. Yes, it was true. We had been trying to conceive for at least five years. And when we finally did get pregnant, it ended in miscarriage. Somehow the idea that Deb was pregnant again, while we remained childless, seemed wrong. It just wasn't fair.

When everyone had left and I returned to my office, the full impact of the situation hit me. How could Deb be having another baby when it seemed she couldn't control or even feed the ones she already had? Why would God give her *another* child and not give us one? Where was the justice in that? We could offer so much love, attention, discipline—all the right things. We even had two extra bedrooms in our house that stood empty.

With my head in my hands, I questioned God. "What are you thinking, Lord?" I whispered. "If you really are sovereign, if you're really in control of our lives, how can this be?" No answer. I lifted my head, took a deep breath, and stood up. "Forget it. I'm going to go home and take a nap."

But God didn't let me off the hook so easily. The next few days only added to what would soon become a crisis of belief. It seemed that everywhere I turned, I faced what I concluded were the injustices of procreation. I picked up the newspaper and the first headline that jumped out was "Teen Pregnancies Increase . . ." I didn't read the article. I flipped on the evening news only to be confronted with a story about welfare reform. I watched a talk-show host interview single moms on welfare who kept having children so that their benefits would increase. I decided to leave the house to get away from it all. But traveling down Market Street, I noticed what appeared to be a mob of protestors with signs. Oh, great! It was about the new Planned Parenthood building.

Soon it became obvious that God was not going to let me forget about the issue of justice and fairness. Deb and her six (going on seven) children, teen pregnancy, welfare moms, abortions, and unwanted pregnancies—how could God allow such rampant unfairness when good people, faithful Christians even, desperately wanted children to love and care for? Was God really in control? And if so, was he losing it? These questions shook the foundations of my faith to the core. It would have been easier to attribute the seeming injustices to biology or statistics. I knew that one in six couples experience infertility. Maybe we just happened to be number six. Maybe it wasn't God, but bad luck or bad biology.

I couldn't make myself believe it. Something as important as having children couldn't be delegated to a random roll of the dice. My relationship with God depended upon the fact that he loved me and was actively involved in my life. After all, I'd given my life to him years ago in college. "God," I had prayed. "Please take my life and be Lord of it. I give myself to you and to your service—all I am and all I ever hope to become." It seemed such a simple and powerful prayer at the time. But now I wondered what I had gotten myself into. Wasn't the ministry difficult enough without the unfairness of infertility added to it?

It was bad enough that such injustice existed. But at this point it became clear to me that God was putting the injustice directly in my path, so that I couldn't ignore it. Kids in my teen group would have said that "God was getting in my face." What was he trying to teach me, anyway? What possible good could come out of all of this? I decided to do what any good, strong spiritual leader would do—I went home and talked with my wife about it.

"I just don't get it," I said. "Is God unfair or is he just taking a vacation?"

Susan smiled a sad little smile and continued cutting up vegetables for a salad. "What does the Bible say?"

She always asks that. I scowled. "It says God is supposed to be just." Then I rattled off a few verses I'd memorized. " 'He will judge the world in righteousness; he will govern the peoples with justice' (Psalm 9:8). 'For the LORD is righteous, he loves justice; upright men will see his face' (Psalm 11:7). 'The LORD loves righteousness and justice; the earth is full of his unfailing love' (Psalm 33:5)."

Susan glanced at me. "All right, smarty-pants. You get three gold stars. But what does all that mean to us?"

I shook my head. "I wish I knew. If God loves justice, how can he possibly allow our infertility to continue while the world runs amuck with unwanted children, abortions, and teen pregnancies?"

Susan didn't say anything, and the only sound that broke the silence was her chopping. Finally she sighed, and said, "Try Job. If anyone knew about unfairness, he did."

Of course, she was right. As I flipped through the book of Job, I saw that his questions mirrored my own. " 'Does God pervert justice? Does the Almighty pervert what is right?' " (8:3); " 'Though I cry, "I've been wronged!" I get no response; though I call for help, there is no justice' " (19:7).

Unfortunately God didn't give Job, or me, any explanations to our questions of unfairness. He didn't explain evil. He didn't defend his sovereignty. But I saw that there was one thing he did do—he confronted Job with his majesty and power. Job may not have come out of the experience with any answers, but he did emerge with an awesome understanding of God. If anyone could have sung "How Great Thou Art" with feeling and passion, it would have been Job.

I closed my Bible and began to wonder if the solution to my spiritual crisis lay a little closer to home than the big issues of how God ran the world. Perhaps it wasn't about abortion and teen pregnancy. Perhaps it was about me and my relationship with God. Would I still love and follow him even if he never gave us a child? Would I still sing "How Great Thou Art" and mean it, despite the adversity and unfairness of infertility? And more importantly, was God somehow showing himself to me in a new and powerful way through what seemed to be nothing but injustice and pain? Maybe what I needed to do was take my eyes off of other people and focus them on God and what he was doing in me. After all, children are not a *reward* for personal, financial, social, or even spiritual accomplishment. God doesn't hand out babies like prizes to good parents.

Yes, I discovered that infertility is difficult, painful, and confusing. Yes, it brings about questions that I still can't answer. Yet I've come to believe that the solution lies not in philosophy or theology, but in a person—Jesus Christ.

And, like any other crisis of faith, even the seeming unfairness of infertility can be a doorway into a new and deeper love for God—a love based not on what he's given me (or withheld from me), but on how great he truly is.

EIGHTEEN

IF SARAH, WHY NOT ME?

Linda, age 46

Pastor Kline stood behind the pulpit and banged his fist on the lectern. "Sarah and Abraham believed God for a miracle!" he shouted. "And they received one!"

I sank lower in my seat. It felt as if a hundred eyes were boring into the back of my head. Was everyone looking at me? Or was it just my imagination? I opened my Bible and stared blankly at the pages, while Pastor Kline continued to preach about Sarah's miracle baby. And the longer he preached, the more angry I became.

It seemed like I'd heard this story a thousand times before. And each time I heard it, I hated it a little bit more. *Remember Sarah!* friends and family would say in an attempt to encourage me to have faith. Remember Sarah? I wished I could forget her! Sarah had a promise from God that she'd have a son. But I had no such promise. Sarah found her belly rounding with child, even though she was past the age of childbearing. Mine was flat—even though for me, too, it was nearly too late. Sarah snuggled a baby, while my arms remained empty. Sarah was blessed by God, at last. My blessing still hadn't come and probably never would.

That's why Sarah's story didn't encourage my faith but rather made me want to scream, "Okay, then—if Sarah, why not me? Where's my miracle?"

The other stories in Scripture were no help, either. Rebecca, Rachel, Hannah, Elizabeth, all eventually conceived the children they'd longed for. God opened their wombs, but he didn't open mine. Wasn't I pious enough? Didn't I have enough faith?

I rejected the last idea. Despite what Pastor Kline said, I wasn't impressed with Sarah's faith. She doubted, even laughed, when the angel told her she'd have a baby within a year. That didn't sound like miracle-making faith to me. Yet God granted her a son, and Rebecca, and Rachel, and Hannah, and Elizabeth, but not me. Somehow I hadn't made the list.

By the time Pastor Kline finished his sermon, I noticed my fists were clenched into tight balls. The words of the benediction echoed hollowly in my ears as I grabbed my Bible and prepared to make a hasty exit. Then it was over, and I scooted from the pew and headed for the side doors.

"Linda, oh Linda," I heard a voice behind me. Reluctantly I stopped and turned. Meredith, our Sunday school teacher, hurried toward me.

"Wasn't that a wonderful sermon?" she gasped. "I was thinking of you the whole time."

I mumbled something unintelligible, then turned again to leave.

Before I could get away, Meredith patted me on the shoulder. "Jack and I are believing God for a miracle for you, too. You never know. Maybe you'll be a modern-day Sarah."

I suppressed an irritated response. How many times had I heard that? More than I could count. I was sick of it. Sick of Sarah, sick of begging God for a baby, sick of being told to just have faith.

"I gotta go," I managed.

When my husband and I arrived home, I shrugged out of my sweater and shoved my Bible onto the shelf. Then I plopped down on the couch, kicked off my shoes, and grabbed the remote. I flipped from one channel to the next, until I finally settled on an old rerun.

Alan went into our bedroom to change clothes. When he came out a few minutes later, he said, "What's wrong with you today? You looked ready to spit nails all the way home."

"God's love is a sham," I answered.

Alan raised his eyebrows. "Pardon me?"

I crossed my arms in disgust. "Well, it is."

"Why do you say that?"

"He gave Sarah a baby, even though she came right out and laughed at his promise. But I pray and pray and pray. And what happens? Nothing. I don't think he even listens to my prayers. I don't know why I bother. What's the use of praying? I've had it! I don't want to hear about Sarah, or Rachel, or Hannah, or Rebecca, or Elizabeth. In fact, I don't want to hear about God anymore!"

I stormed to the bedroom and slammed the door, leaving my husband stunned at my behavior.

For the next eleven months my Bible remained on the shelf unopened. I quit going to my small group. My prayer journal lay unused, and my church attendance became sporadic at best. When I did go to church, I hated it. People would stand up and give testimonies about how God had blessed them with a raise, or a new job, or their little Suzy with a blue ribbon at the state fair, or healing for their Aunt Matilda's arthritis in her left knee. "God is so good," they'd say.

And all the while my jaw grew tighter and my face became redder. *God is good?* I'd shout in my mind. *I don't think so. At least not to me. What kind of God would help Suzy win a blue ribbon but turn his back when I ask him to heal my infertility?* With that thought, I shut the door more firmly on my relationship with God. I didn't want to talk about him, I didn't want to read about him, and I certainly didn't want to pray to him. I just wanted to be left alone.

Then one day while cleaning out the closet in our spare bedroom, I found a box filled with college treasures. There was a small book with peonies on the cover. I opened it and discovered pages and pages filled with my own writing. I sat on the floor with my back against the closet door and turned to the first page. The purple heading read "Junior Year." It was the year after I'd accepted Christ. I flipped to about halfway through and began to read:

> *I saw the sunrise today, Lord. I wish I could say it was because I was up early to pray, but as you know, I had to pull an all-nighter to get that paper done. But it was worth it to see the streaks of orange, red, and gold at the dawn of a new day. I stood there and thought to myself, I know the Guy who made that sunrise. He lives in me. You know, I can feel you there, Lord, in my heart. Some days, like today, your love is a tangible thing, like a warm blanket that wraps around my insides. In these moments, I feel like I should shout to the stars about what an awesome, incredible, super-Wow God you are. I can't believe there was ever a time when I turned my back on you. What a fool I was. But everything's different now, God. My life, my heart, is filled with the wonder of knowing you. I'll never forget this feeling. I'll never forget to keep on loving you. I promise. . . .*

Tears came to my eyes as I read the words and remembered the day I had written them. I remembered how nothing else had mattered as much as knowing and loving God. But a lot had changed since then. Too much.

I sat there with my journal resting against my knees and realized how much I missed my relationship with God. There was a loneliness in me that went deeper than not having children. In these last months I'd lost something even more precious than my hope for a child. I'd lost my closeness with God. Yet despite this realization, I knew that my anger remained in me like a huge stone, trapping me, holding me back. Only God could free me.

Slowly I stood up and pulled a pen from the top drawer of the desk. Then I reached up and grabbed a blank journal from the shelf above it. I sat down at my desk and began to write: *God, it's me, Linda. I'm mad at you.*

I wrote for an hour, pouring out my bitterness, my anger, my hurt. And in so doing, I began the long, slow journey back to God, a journey that has still not ended. But on the way, I'm finding that God understands my anger, my pain. He's not threatened by my honesty.

Now as I begin to look again at the stories of Sarah, Rebecca, Rachel, Elizabeth, and Hannah, I'm starting to see them in a new light. I see that each woman had her own unique life path. Sarah's was different from Rachel's. Rebecca's from Hannah's and Elizabeth's. And mine is different, too. Unique. I can't compare what God did for others with what he's done or will do for me, because my life's purpose is different from theirs. But one thing is the same for all the biblical women—each of their lives fit into the larger story of the kingdom of God. Each had her place in the bigger picture.

So as I continue to make my way back to God, I'm beginning to wonder if the question for me is not so much if his plan will someday lead to children, but rather how this life of mine fits into the whole of God's kingdom. Somehow I think that may be the question that really matters. It could be the question I must answer if I'm ever to find peace.

Today, as the months go by and my potential childbearing days are gone, I'm discovering that it's good to wrestle with God for the answers I need. It's good to cry out to him, to keep turning to him with all my doubts, my anger, and my pain. It's better to shout at him than to be silent, better to call him unkind than not to call on him at all.

And in this quest I'm finding that God does not condemn me for my doubts. He doesn't expect me to be happy about my infertility. All he asks is that I bring my anger to him. He can handle it. He has big shoulders, as big as the sunrise.

He Is There

When dreams are as dying things
Withering in your grasp,
When hope becomes a stranger
In a parched, desolate land,
When vision has all but vanished
As mist before the fire,
He is there.
When prayers crumble at your feet
In wisps of shattered words,
When night gathers dark and deep
Shrouding trails of light,
When all seems lost forever
As if day will never dawn,
He is there.
When you look deep inside
And see the barren soil,
When despair has gained mastery
And tears have all run dry,
When there's no one left, nothing left
But the bitter taste of death,
He is there.
As He was in Gethsemane
The night before the trial,
As He was at Calvary
When nails were driven deep,
As He lay within the tomb
Before the dawn of life,
He is there.

NINETEEN

WHY IS THIS HAPPENING TO ME? AM I BEING PUNISHED?

Samantha, age 36

The stars are beautiful over Yosemite National Park. They shine like a thousand diamonds, especially on clear winter nights when the air is crisp, the snow fresh fallen, and the pines are covered with mantles of white. It was just such a night when I sat on the porch of our tiny rented cabin and contemplated the "whys" of the universe.

Josh and I had come to Yosemite to escape the pressures of seemingly endless infertility treatments. We needed relief from the hold-your-breath hopes and crushing disappointments, a reprieve from the pills, charts, needles, and schedules. Here, in our favorite winter vacation spot, I planned to forget, at least for a while, that I was childless at age thirty-four, that God was letting my reproductive years slip by without the baby we longed for. But tonight the questions and the doubts would not be silenced. In the quiet of the winter evening, they whispered to me: *Why hasn't God blessed us? Why has he turned his back on us?*

In the midst of my thoughts, the silence was broken by the sound of a child's laughter. I looked across the way to see a little girl scampering down the path, her boots shiny in the light of the quarter moon. She wore big woolen gloves and a down coat so puffy that she was practically lost in its marshmallow folds. Behind her an older boy dragged a bright red toboggan. His face was half hidden beneath the flaps of an oversized hat, so all that could be seen were the white puffs of his breath on the cold air. Farther down the path, their parents walked arm in arm, smiling as they watched their children head for the cabin three doors down.

With a loud creak, the door opened behind me, and my husband stepped onto the porch. "Nice night," he commented.

I glanced up at him, watching as he, too, was drawn to the family on the path. Without a word, he pulled up a second chair and sat beside me.

He would have made such a good father, I thought. He was a kind man, loving, godly. And he was wonderful with kids. There was no one our nieces and nephews liked better than "Uncle Joshie." So why did God continue to deny him children of his own? Was it my fault?

Josh gestured toward the people on the path. "I always thought that would be us," he said.

I looked again at the little family. The girl had already reached the cabin, flung open the door, and disappeared inside. The boy was close behind her.

I sighed. "Yeah, me too," I said, just as the father and mother reached the turn in the path that led to their cabin. In a moment they were inside.

Then there was nothing left to see or hear, except the soft thump of snow falling from the branches of the trees and the occasional chirp of a blue jay as it hopped across the snow.

A half hour went by before Josh said he was cold and headed back inside.

"I'll come in in a minute," I said.

The door closed with a quiet thud, and I was alone again, more alone, it seemed, than I'd ever been before. The silence, the darkness, wrapped around me like a cloak, and then the questions began again. Why weren't Josh and I like that family? Why did God refuse to bless us with children? What had I done wrong? I needed to find an answer; I needed to find something that would solve the problem of "why." Then an answer came, the same one that had been floating around in my head for months—but this time it lodged in my heart like a sharp thorn. *Perhaps God is punishing me.*

I thought back to the years before I was married, before I'd become a Christian. I was sexually active then, even though I knew it was wrong. Perhaps I was reaping the punishment for those promiscuous years. Or maybe God had really been trying to protect me from getting pregnant back then, so he made me infertile. But now, when I wanted kids, I couldn't have any.

Or maybe God was punishing me for waiting until we had settled into our careers before we started trying to have a baby. If I hadn't been so selfish, if I'd tried sooner, would we have a baby now? Was God simply saying, "Sorry, you're too late"?

I groaned. I'd done plenty of things that God could be punishing me for. So which was it? My lack of sexual purity as a young person, my desire for financial security before we started trying to conceive, or something else that I didn't even remember? Of course, sin sometimes has natural consequences that hinder fertility. If I had contracted a sexually transmitted disease or had had an abortion that scarred my tubes, then I might simply be suffering the effects of my mistakes. But neither of those things had happened. Still, if I could only pin down the past sin that was responsible for this problem, I was sure I'd feel better, at least a little bit.

The only problem with my theory, of course, was that I knew plenty of women who'd been sexually active before marriage, who'd waited before having children, even women who'd had abortions and affairs. Yet they weren't infertile. So what made me different? Why was God punishing me while giving them the children they wanted? Even though it didn't make sense, my feelings of guilt remained.

A breeze rustled through the branches overhead and dropped a clump of snow onto the plank in front of me. I watched the ice splatter on the wood and skitter beneath my chair. A chill raced through me. I rose and paced up and down the porch. Then another thought came to mind and stuck. *What if God isn't punishing me for past sins but protecting me from future ones?*

After all, the Bible tells me that God knows my innermost thoughts, my comings and goings, when I sit down and when I rise up. Maybe God knew that I wouldn't be a good mother. Maybe he wasn't allowing me to get pregnant because of how poor I would be at the whole thing. He could be punishing me for my lack of patience, my temper, my frivolousness. But I knew then and I know now that God is good. I know he blesses his children. So, I reasoned, I must have done something to block his goodness. I must not be deserving of a child. That was it! God knew something awful about me, either in my past, my present, or my future, something that made me unworthy to be a parent.

I looked up at the bright slice of the moon overhead. Somehow my "answers" didn't make me feel any better. Who was this God I served and loved, and who was I in relation to him? Those, perhaps, were the questions that really needed answering. "But not tonight," I murmured as I reached for the doorknob.

The next day Josh and I hiked to the bottom of Lower Yosemite Falls. Sunlight danced off the water to make a thousand tiny rainbows, each brilliant with a spectrum of color. I stood with my hands resting on the railing of the small wooden bridge, while the falls formed tiny ice crystals that caught in the breeze and landed in a heap on the rocks below. The scene was breathtaking, and I was reminded again that God had made all this beauty—but he had not made a child for Josh and me. And with that thought my mind again ran to ideas from the night before. Were all my excuses, all my reasons for God's actions correct? Was God really like that? Did he withhold blessings for mistakes I'd made in the past or for character flaws I had now?

I turned to Josh. "Do you think God is punishing me?"

Josh gave me a blank stare. "What are you talking about?"

"The reason we don't have children. Do you think God is punishing me?"

"That's ridiculous."

"Is it?"

Josh's eyebrows arched to his hairline. "Okay, Zophar, whatever you say."

"Who?"

"One of Job's friends. That's the reason he gave for Job's misfortune."

"So it *is* in the Bible. I knew it!"

Josh shook his head. "You know better than that. I'd say it's not God you're having a problem with, but yourself."

"What do you mean?"

Josh turned and stared at the bottom of the falls. "I've been watching you for months now, trying to dig up some reason for why we aren't getting pregnant. You think that if you can just figure it out, it will somehow not hurt so much. Well," his knuckles turned pale as he gripped the railing tighter, "maybe there is no reason why, at least none that we can understand. We'll probably never come up with a tidy little answer to attach to our lack of children. So the question is, why are you so desperate to find one?" Josh's voice grew louder. "What if God just says no, and that's it? What are you going to do then? What if there is no *why*?"

I took a step backward, surprised at the severity of Josh's tone and his words. "I-I don't know," I sputtered.

"Well, you'd better figure it out," he said, then pulled his coat tighter around his neck and headed back up the trail.

I stood there watching his back as he retreated. Behind me, the river gurgled and gulped as it sped beneath the bridge, and the falls tumbled down with a muted roar. But nothing was as loud as the sound of Josh's last question still ringing in my ears. *What if there is no why?*

The idea formed in my stomach like a cold knot. And slowly, as I stood on the bridge with the icy falls spraying tiny droplets of mist all around me, I realized the truth. Without a "why" I would have nothing left to fight against the fury that welled up inside of me. I needed to give God an excuse for denying me a child. I needed to place the blame on me. If I didn't, my anger would turn toward God, and that was a possibility that scared me more than the guilt of my past sins.

But Josh was right. It was time to face my fears. I had to examine why I felt so bad about myself that I interpreted suffering as deserved punishment. I had to discover why I was so afraid to confront God with my frustration and my anger. Did I have such a low view of myself that I thought God would reject me or stop loving me if I gave him the slightest reason to do so?

In the next several months as I wrote in my journal and studied the Old and New Testaments, I discovered a God who not only endures but welcomes the honest expression of our feelings and doubts. I found a God in Job, Jonah, and Habakkuk who responds to those who seek him, even to those who seek him in frustration and anger. There I saw a God who confronts our "whys" not with answers but with himself, with the glory and wonder of his unchanging character.

Later, in the Gospels, I encountered a God who loves me unconditionally, who not only forgives my sins but also forgets them. And in the Psalms I found a way to express my frustration so that I was always brought back to the person of God. "How long, O Lord," I cried from Psalm 13, "will you forget me forever?" And there I was reminded again to trust in his unfailing love and to rejoice in his salvation.

Finally, in the story of a man born blind, I discovered my "why." There I read, "Neither this man nor his parents sinned . . . but this happened so that the work of God might be displayed in his life" (John 9:3). Could I, too, be satisfied with that answer and no more?

Today I can say that I still don't know why God has not given us a child. I may never know. But I no longer feel as if I must come up with a reason to get him off the hook. I just need to keep seeking him, keep expressing my hurt and frustration, and keep telling him how I feel. In the end I can only hope that through this suffering God's work might somehow be displayed in my life. Perhaps that is answer enough.

TWENTY

OF IDOLS AND
FALSE GODS

Mara, age 33

"The Israelites secretly did things against the LORD their God that were not right. From watchtower to fortified city they built themselves high places in all their towns. They set up sacred stones and Asherah poles on every high hill and under every spreading tree. . . . The LORD warned Israel and Judah. . . . But they would not listen and were as stiff-necked as their fathers, who did not trust in the LORD their God. . . . They forsook all the commands of the LORD their God and made for themselves two idols cast in the shape of calves, and an Asherah pole. They bowed down to all the starry hosts, and they worshiped Baal. . . . So the LORD was very angry with Israel and . . . the people of Israel were taken from their homeland into exile in Assyria, and they are still there" (2 Kings 17:9–23, selected verses).

I shook my head and closed my Bible. *Those foolish Israelites,* I thought. If I'd seen all the miracles they'd seen, if I'd witnessed fire from heaven coming down to burn up a soaked offering, and if I'd heard God speak through the prophets, I certainly wouldn't be putting up any Asherah poles or bowing down to any Baals. What was wrong with those people?

I frowned, then looked out the living room window. A row of yellow daffodils lifted their teacup heads to peek just above the sill. I smiled at them. Daffodils were my favorite. Beyond them, a red-breasted robin hopped across the grass and perched on the short brick wall that surrounded my rose garden. My gaze traveled over the pink, red, and lavender roses cascading over the wall. Such a beautiful scene, yet somehow it failed to provide me with the sense of peace I longed for.

I sighed and rose from the couch. There was so much to do today. Besides my eight-hour workday, I wanted to search the Internet for a new infertility treatment I'd heard about, try to figure out how to get enough money for another procedure, organize my temperature charts, and go to Wal-Mart to buy an ovulation predictor kit. At noon Jake and I had another appointment at the infertility clinic. I placed my Bible on the coffee table and called upstairs to Jake.

"What's up?" he asked as he came down the stairs rubbing his eyes and then adjusting his tie.

"Don't forget our appointment at the clinic today."

"Another appointment? What's it for this time?"

"We need to schedule the next procedure."

"But we can't afford another procedure."

I felt my blood pressure rise. I took a deep breath. Stress wasn't good for egg production. "I'll find a way."

Jake rolled his eyes. "Whatever."

I snapped. "What's wrong with you? All I want is a little support. I'm trying to have this baby for both of us." Soon I was shouting at him. "After I've gone through all this, you're telling me you don't want a child? How can you say 'whatever' like it doesn't matter? Don't you know how much this means to me? Don't you care?"

He opened his mouth to respond, but I didn't give him the chance.

"Well, fine. I'll go to the appointment by myself. I don't need you anyway. There's plenty of donor sperm out there." I stormed out of the room, not caring that I had lost my temper again, not caring that I'd hurt the man I love.

As I turned to go into the kitchen, I could see that Jake was stunned and frustrated. After a moment I heard his footsteps on the stairs again. Ten minutes later he came back down and went out the door without a word. He was gone.

I held my face in my hands. Why had I said those awful things to Jake? Why couldn't I control my feelings, and my words? It was this infertility thing. It was making me crazy. But a baby would fix all that. Once I had a child, everything would be all right again. I just knew it.

The morning at work crept by slower than a snail. At noon I headed for the clinic. Jake was waiting for me in the parking lot.

"Hey," he said, his voice cautious.

"Hey," I said back. I lifted one hand and tucked a stray strand of hair behind my ear. "Look, about earlier . . ." I paused, trying to phrase it right, "I didn't mean what I said. I was just nervous about this appointment, that's all."

Jake looked at me and didn't say anything. I could tell what he was thinking. *Whatever.* We walked to the door, and Jake opened it for me. I took a deep breath and walked in.

Twenty minutes later we were sitting in the doctor's office talking to the man who had become an intimate part of our lives over the last few years. The doctor looked at me and shook his head. "I really don't think zygote intrafallopian transfer is going to work any better than the two in vitro fertilizations or the gamete intrafallopian transfer you've already done."

I felt my chest constrict. "Then what are we going to do?" I said. "I want a baby!"

"I know, Mara." The doctor walked around his desk and sat on the corner. He put his hand on my shoulder. "I know this is hard to hear.

But in my professional opinion, I think you should discontinue treatment."

My heart sank. "What?"

"Perhaps you and Jake should consider adoption."

"I don't want to adopt! I want my own baby!"

The doctor glanced at Jake, and Jake looked at me. "Honey, I think the doctor is saying it's time to move on."

I glared at him. "We can go to another doctor. Ann went to another clinic, and she got pregnant."

"You know there's no way we can afford another procedure anyway."

"I'll get the money from my brother."

"We've already borrowed from your sister and your mom, and we can't pay them back. I don't want to borrow anymore."

Tears welled in my eyes. "Don't you understand? I want a baby. I'll do whatever it takes." I turned to the doctor again. "ZIFT, another IVF... I just need to know what to do. Something has to work!"

The doctor put a hand to his forehead. "I'm sorry, Mara. There's nothing else *I* can do."

"You just don't care about us anymore." I could hear my voice rising, but I couldn't stop it. I clenched my fists and stared at the doctor through tear-filled eyes. "You're afraid your statistics will go down if we fail again. Well, I don't care about that. If you won't do another procedure, I'll go somewhere else." I grabbed my purse and left the office as quickly as I could.

I sat in my car for five minutes before Jake came out. He opened the passenger side door and climbed in beside me. We sat there together— silently—for what seemed like an eternity. Finally, Jake turned toward me. "What's happening to you? I don't know who you are anymore." His voice was quiet.

I leaned against the headrest and closed my eyes. "You just don't understand how much I *need* this baby. It's like an ache inside that only a baby can fill."

"God is supposed to fill us, Mara, not a child."

"I know. But I still want a baby."

"So do I."

Jake remained in the car for a few minutes more, then opened the door and got out. "I've got to get back to work," he muttered. "We'll talk about this tonight at home."

But we didn't talk about it that night. Instead, I called my brother and asked him for a loan. "Sorry, sis," he said, "I don't have that kind of money. And if I did, I'd buy a new car for Sue."

"A new car?" I responded. "You think a car is more important than a baby?"

"Come on, that's not fair. Besides, I don't have a penny to spare."

"Oh, all right. I'll talk to you later." I hung up the phone and stared at the books on the shelf above the TV. Five books on infertility, three on pregnancy, and one titled *The Complete Book of Baby Names*. And the worst part was, I'd read every one of them from cover to cover. In fact, I'd read a couple of them twice. I'd done everything I could think of to accomplish the goal of having a baby. Nothing had worked.

I threw my head back. "Why won't you give me a baby?" I cried to God. He was silent. He seemed to always be silent these days—in my morning devotions, in my evening prayer times, at the altar at church. Sometimes I wondered if he even heard my prayers.

The next day I called another fertility doctor and told him my story. He, too, said that further treatment would likely be unsuccessful. So I called a third doctor. He agreed to treat us, though he didn't think the results would be any different. But I was willing to try. I just needed the money.

That day a notice came in the mail. *"You've been preapproved for $10,000 credit,"* it read. *"At only 2.9% interest."* I grabbed the application, ignoring the small print that read "introductory rate." A week later the new Visa card arrived. A week after that I applied for a MasterCard with a $4,000 credit limit. Now I had enough to pay for another procedure. I called and made the appointment. My husband, who thought the money had come from my brother, agreed to give it one more try. So, with my hopes soaring as high as my credit card debt, we underwent ZIFT, where the doctor fertilized my eggs with Jake's sperm, then placed the zygotes into my fallopian tube. Following the procedure, I waited two long weeks, counting the days, counting the hours. This time, I thought, it had to work. It just had to!

Yet that time of month came right on schedule. I wasn't pregnant. The procedure had failed. What would I do now? There was nothing left to try, nothing left to do. *It can't be the end*, I told myself. I couldn't endure it if it was. Surely there was something else I could do to make this pregnancy thing work. I would do anything. Anything at all.

Anything? The question haunted me. We were already deep in debt, our marriage was in trouble, and my life lay in shambles. Yet I couldn't let go of my need to have a child. It drove me; it consumed me. And now there was nothing left on which to place my hope.

For days I walked around in a fog, stumbling through life like a woman drunk on despair. Jake watched me warily. I could tell he was worried, but he didn't dare ask the questions I knew were on his mind. Would depression consume me? Would I always have this dour look on my face? Would I ever get past this place of pain? And always it came back to the question of what I would do next.

Finally an answer came, completely unexpected. One day I was flipping through my Bible, looking for a verse quoted by our pastor in his Sunday sermon. But instead my eyes caught the passage from 2 Kings 17: "They set up sacred stones and Asherah poles on every high hill and under every spreading tree . . . [and] did not trust in the LORD their God."

As I read on, the words cut through me like a knife, revealing, in all-too-sudden clarity, the depth of my need, my pain, my sin. *Perhaps,* I thought, *the Israelites weren't so crazy after all.* I saw them in a new light. And I saw myself in them.

I took a deep breath and reread the passage. Slowly I closed the Bible. Asherah poles and statues of Baal. How was my desperation any different from theirs? Like the Israelites, I understood that procreation was an important part of life, yet God didn't always give children for a prayer. And I, too, had turned elsewhere for answers. They set up Asherah poles and prayed for pregnancy; I searched the Internet and put my trust in the next procedure. They bowed down to Baal to increase their fertility; I bowed to medicine and the false power of my own will. Their statues were made of stone, mine were made of a desire so strong that it may as well have been a stone within me. Sure, I kept praying to God; I never stopped my morning devotions. But God wasn't first in my life. My hoped-for baby had taken his place.

As the truth washed through me, I felt my heart breaking for the hundredth time, only now it was different. This time I knew I had to change, but I didn't know how.

Again I cried out to God. "I give up," I prayed. "But I can't give up. I can't let go." I looked down at my white-knuckled fists. They clung so tightly to my desire for a baby, I couldn't release the need.

I grimaced and dropped my head. "Help me, Lord," I whispered. Then I waited. Nothing happened. I waited longer. Still nothing. The pain, the desperation, the need, remained.

The next day, and the next, and the next, I repeated my prayer. I brought my tight fists to God and waited for something to change. Still nothing did. Had God forgotten me? Had he abandoned me? I thought so, until three weeks later.

I sat in the back pew at church with my heart as heavy as lead in my chest. Then the choir began to sing, "All to Jesus, I surrender, all to Him I freely give. . . ." As the words flowed over me, heaven finally broke through. I felt the hand of God reaching down, deep within me, freeing me from my need to conceive. In my mind, I could see my fists opening at last, releasing the desperation, letting go of the idols of fertility. In those moments, God worked a miracle in my heart, doing for me what I couldn't do for myself. He cleansed me of my idolatry and restored my devotion to him alone.

Then, as the song came to an end, I began to laugh, a soft chuckle filled with a newfound joy. And that's when I knew that now, whatever happened, whether I had a baby or not, I would be okay. God had finally set me free.

In the months that followed, those around me began to see the change. I still hoped for a baby, but the desperation was gone. I smiled more. I even laughed at my husband's jokes. And mostly, my prayer life became a time of joy, of peace. No longer did the idols of fertility stand between me and God. I could sense him again there with me, caring for me.

Eventually, as I drew closer to God and he to me, I began to understand that he had given me something even greater than a baby. He had given me himself. And nothing was worth losing the love we share.

A Word
of Hope

TWENTY-ONE

TREASURES FROM THE HOUSE OF POVERTY

Bryan, age 35

I have found that the Christian life is full of lessons about God and his character. Often we learn through the hearing and study of the Word. Sometimes we experience tragedy or failure, and this brings us closer to Christ. Other lessons are learned over a period of years and in many stages. They require a deeper study and understanding of God's Word and how it relates to our personal lives. They require interaction with God through prayer. Often, they require us to struggle with God. The story of Bethany is such a lesson. Her story doesn't begin with infertility, nor does it end with her birth. Nor does this story begin and end with us. It is as old as Scripture itself. It is the story of poverty—a story of taking up the cross of Christ.

We live in a world of utilitarian love. Marriage relationships often last only as long as both parties benefit. Business relationships strive for win-

win scenarios. Most family relationships rely on blood and genetics (how many of us would visit our relatives if they weren't related to us?). But God's love is different. He doesn't love us because of what we can do for him. He loves us even though it cost him his life.

But what about us? What about our love for him? What do we mean when we sing, "Oh, how I love Jesus" or "I love you, Lord, and I lift my voice"? Scripture teaches us that we love him because he first loved us. But it also asks the question, "Would you love God if everything you had were taken away?" More personally, "Is my love for God dependent upon my benefiting from the relationship? Or can I love God independently of all he has given me?" That is the question God asked me to answer through our struggle with infertility.

Our story is not much different than those of most other couples who experience difficulty conceiving. We assumed we'd get pregnant soon after we started trying, but we didn't. Eventually we had some tests done through our local OB/GYN. Later we went to an infertility specialist and had more tests and procedures done. But we remained childless.

Before we discovered our infertility, I thought I was a pretty spiritual guy. I'd been a Christian forever. I was a licensed minister soon to be ordained. I led worship at my local church and taught the adult Sunday school class. I was taking classes at Fuller Theological Seminary and working toward a Master of Divinity degree. I had all my theological ducks in a row and thought my faith was strong. But the experience of infertility shook the foundation of my relationship with God. After years of trying and praying with no success, I questioned his sovereignty in my life. And eventually I began to seriously question his love for me and for my wife. We'd tried for so long, hoped for so long, prayed for so long. But God continued to ignore our pleas. In a way I felt like a child who had made a special gift for Dad only to have him disregard it. This was not the God I knew from Scripture. Yet I also knew that many of the great men and women of the Bible encountered the same feeling of abandonment. For them, and for us, there were more questions than answers.

Did God really care about me? Did he really desire to bless me, or was life one big disciplinary lesson? If that was God's love, maybe I needed to reconsider whether I wanted to be a part of it.

Like many of my Christian friends, I had been conditioned to correlate God's love with personal blessing. I'd participated in testimony services that were filled with people thanking God for all the physical blessings they'd received. Someone would stand up and thank God for a new job. Someone else would thank the Lord for meeting a financial need. And still another would praise God for his family.

But I asked, *What about the man who lost his job or didn't have a family? What about the man whose family was taken from him? Could he stand up and praise God? Could I stand and praise him? Why didn't anyone ever jump up and say, "Praise God! I've had a really tough year."* Of course, I knew the one thing I could always be thankful for: Christ died for me, and I have eternal life. But that fact seemed intangible amid the pain and suffering of infertility.

As I was questioning God's love for me, however, God was setting me up to deal with my love for him. As I would soon discover, it was only through challenging my love for him that I would be able to truly see his love for me.

My wife and I had been married for eleven years. We had been waiting all those years for the children we were now thinking we'd never have. Eleven years is a long time. Too long to wait. Too long to hope. So on that third Sunday of May, the Sunday when mothers are honored, I had no idea the day would be the turning point in my life and in my relationship with God.

As anyone experiencing infertility knows, Mother's Day is usually the worst day of the year. No other day so painfully underscores the lack, the ache, the emptiness of not being able to have children. No other day makes it so clear that where others are blessed, we are not. Of course, I understood that we were in no way close to experiencing loss like Job or, for that matter, many other people. We had good friendships, a nice home, cars that worked, and family that loved us. But on this particular day that celebrated parenthood and honored mothers, we were in complete poverty. There were no small, smiling faces to greet us with love and appreciation. There were no cards or gifts. No kisses from little lips or hugs from little arms. There was only a constant reminder that this house of poverty was our home.

That morning I stared blankly at the tiny red needle bouncing back and forth on my electronic tuner. It was easier to tune my guitar than to think of all this day meant to my wife, and therefore to me. All the songs had been rehearsed, and the entire worship team was assembled, waiting for the service to begin. In a moment I would have to lead the congregation in worship. But first, the pastor would greet the people with a huge smile and a "Happy Mother's Day!" Roses would be passed out. Special gifts would be given to the oldest mother, the newest mother, the mother of the most kids, the grandmother of the most grandkids, and so on. All this would be no problem for me, but it would be for Michelle. I could even plow through the worship set with the appropriate amount of enthusiasm and a sufficient smile—no problem. But Michelle would sit near the back of the church inconspicuously, hoping that no one would notice her, like she did every year. And every year my heart broke for her.

So as I sat there waiting for the time of worship to begin, I started to pray, not for a child (I had long ago stopped praying that way—God knew the desire of my heart), but that God would somehow reveal his love for us, and in particular for Michelle. Especially now, especially today.

The service began just as I expected it would. The pastor gave his "Happy Mother's Day" greeting, and the women marched up to the front of the church for their roses and gifts.

This year, though, the Mother's Day theatrics seemed longer than ever before. I purposely avoided eye contact with my wife. I could feel her emotions and I knew her thoughts. Finally we began the worship portion of the service. I planned to hurry through the songs in an effort to get through the day. The sermon would be on Proverbs 31, and that would be enough to endure.

So we began the music, and, unexpectedly, I felt the presence of God in an unusual way. I didn't sense his moving through the congregation as much as I felt the Holy Spirit moving in my heart. He caught me by surprise, since I was not in a state of mind to truly worship him. I had not prepared my heart. I had not purposely focused on him. But he met me in what became one of the most moving worship experiences of my life. Through the music and lyrics God called me to abandon my conditional love for him. He asked me to be the one to stand up and proclaim, "Praise God! This has been a tough eleven years." He challenged me to let go of my doubts.

Finally the last hymn began: "My Jesus, I love Thee. I know Thou art mine." The sound swelled around me, and I knew that this song would be the climax of my worship experience. I had not chosen the hymn for this purpose. In fact, I'd picked it only because we hadn't sung it for months.

The music flowed over me like a warm shower after a long day at work. But the words penetrated my soul even deeper—God called me to proclaim my love for him today, of all days. If only Michelle could be a part of what he was doing in me. If only she, too, could feel his presence and be assured of his love.

As we sang the chorus, I glanced in her direction and couldn't believe my eyes. There was my quiet, conservative wife, with both arms raised high, her eyes closed, and a huge smile on her face as she belted out the words: "If ever I loved Thee, my Jesus, 'tis now." Wonder washed over me. God had broken through.

We didn't speak much on the way home. In fact, the rest of the day was normal. But I knew something had changed in my wife's heart. I knew that somehow, through the Mother's Day service—in spite of the Mother's Day service—God had reached down and healed her. He had shown her, and shown me as well, how to praise him from the house of poverty. By the grace of God, he brought us to the place of being able to love him not because of what he had given us but in spite of what he had kept from us. And so we discovered that the house of poverty held the greatest treasure of all.

That night we lay in bed looking at the ceiling. Shadows from the tree outside played over the rough surface. The gentle tick of my alarm clock was the only sound to break the silence. I rolled over and looked at my wife beside me. "You know," I said, "I think you should take a pregnancy test tomorrow."

"Hmmm," Michelle responded. "I'm not late yet."

"I know," I said. "But you should take the test anyway."

"Okay."

The next morning, I climbed out of the shower and reached for my towel. "Look near my sink," Michelle called from the other room as she was making the bed. Her voice was calm, with just a twist of humor. Her tone gave no indication as to what I would find.

So I looked next to her sink and saw a fat plastic stick. I picked it up. There, in the tiny window, was a pink plus sign. I looked again. The plus sign remained. "Does this mean what I think it means?" I asked.

Michelle laughed. "Yes. Can you believe it? After all these years."

I looked at the pregnancy test stick for the third time and chuckled at God's timing. Then I took the stick and walked into the bedroom, holding it up for her to see. "Positive." I shook my head.

She grinned.

It was odd that in those moments there were no cheers or shouts of joy. Instead, we just looked at each other and smiled with an understanding that could only have come after a carefully timed course of events orchestrated by a sovereign God. The day after Mother's Day, the very day after we'd learned to praise and love him from within our house of poverty, is when we found out that we were going to have our miracle baby at last. How could I have ever doubted God's sovereignty in my life? I would never be able to question it again.

As I look back, I marvel that God took us both, on a day that represented our poverty, and enabled us to love him. And all the while, Bethany was already there. God could hardly wait to take us to a new understanding of him so that he could richly bless us not only with a baby but also with a deeper relationship with him.

Bethany is nearly four months old now. We thank God for her every time we see her, every time we hold her, every time we change her little diaper. But unlike other parents, she also reminds us that our love for God doesn't require his blessing of children. We see God's love for us in her eyes. We see his longing for us in her smile. We hear his grace when we say her name, because her name—Bethany—means house of poverty.

TWENTY-TWO

HEAVEN'S GIFT

Vanessa, age 47

"Surprise! You're infertile!" my gynecologist said to me one day when I was in for my yearly exam. Well, she didn't actually say that, but she might as well have.

I was lying in that most uncomfortable position, while the doctor poked around with her cold instruments. I stared at the ceiling and gripped the thin tissue sheet that was supposed to cover me.

"So do you see anything odd down there?" I asked.

The doctor glanced up. "Everything looks fine," she said, then looked at me more closely. "Why? Have you been experiencing anything that I should know about?"

"No, not really," I answered. "It's just that Steve and I have been trying to get pregnant."

She gave a thoughtful "hmmm" and continued her prodding.

I tried not to squirm.

She held up a long stick that looked like an overgrown Q-tip. "You can sit up now."

I breathed a sigh of relief and pushed myself up, being careful to grab the pink tissue sheet and tuck it in around me.

"So how long have you been trying to get pregnant?" she asked, as she pulled off her thin rubber gloves.

"Oh, about a year and a half."

She paused and examined me for a moment with her eyes. I could tell what she was thinking. I felt a little colder and tugged at the tissue again.

"You know," she said finally, "infertility is defined as a year of unprotected sex without conception. You may want to consider having some tests done."

The tissue tore in my hand.

Infertility? Tests? I swallowed. "Uh . . . but, oh, are you sure?"

She shrugged her shoulders. "You said it has been over a year?"

"Yes, but—"

"But?"

"Maybe our timing has been off."

"Maybe," she answered, but I could tell she didn't believe it. I cringed.

"Still, if you're serious about getting pregnant," she continued, "I'd highly recommend the tests."

I swallowed again, hard, then took a deep breath before answering. "Okay, if you say so. What do I need to do?"

She picked up her pencil and scribbled something on a sheet of paper. "Not just you, Steve too."

I grimaced. Steve was going to hate this.

The doctor watched me for a moment. When I didn't say anything, she nodded once and continued writing. "I'm ordering the preliminary tests. How does next week sound for you?"

And so began the journey that would last for the next eight years. During that time we had enough tests and procedures to make me feel like a human pincushion, as well as two miscarriages and numerous heartbreaks.

We were about to consider in vitro fertilization when a call came from my husband's twenty-two-year-old cousin.

She asked for Steve, and I handed him the phone. After about forty-five seconds, a startled expression crossed his face, followed by eager anticipation. His eyes met mine. "We'll take the baby!" he nearly shouted into the receiver.

My hand flew to his arm. "What's going on?" I mouthed the question.

He put his palm over the lower half of the receiver and quickly whispered, "Shanna's pregnant. She says she doesn't want the baby. She was planning to abort, but she'll have the baby if we want to adopt it."

My mouth fell open. "Is she serious?"

He nodded, then spoke into the receiver again. "Yes, yes, absolutely. That'll be no problem. Just send us the bills." He paused while Shanna spoke on the other end of the line. Steve grabbed my hand in his and grinned. "Okay, then, we'll talk to you again later," he said into the phone. "Take care now. And thank you. Thank you so much." He hung up.

"Can you believe it?" he said to me as he turned, grabbed me, and swung me into the air. "We're going to have a baby at last!"

But I wasn't so sure. After two miscarriages, I knew how attached a woman could become to the baby growing in her womb. Still, I laughed with him and wondered, *Could this be it, Lord?*

In the following months as Shanna grew larger and larger, so did our hopes. Steve's family was so excited for us. They began buying baby clothes and planning a party for the new arrival. Shanna was pleased, too. Despite my doubts, she continued to reassure me that everything was going to happen as planned. She called every week with updates and always told me about her doctor visits. I went in with her to her twenty-two-week ultrasound appointment and saw the baby for the first time— a little girl. The sight brought tears to my eyes. *Will that be my baby, Lord?*

The baby was due in September, and somewhere around mid-July I started to really believe that this was going to end happily for us, that we would finally have a baby of our own. I began to plan the nursery and buy pink little girl things to decorate it.

Then, three weeks before the baby was due, Shanna called again. When she asked for Steve, I knew something was wrong. He took the phone, and immediately his features hardened into a look of pain. After a minute he hung up the phone and turned to me. "She says she's keeping the baby."

The words dug into my heart like talons. Steve gathered me in his arms. We stood there, too hurt to cry, too stunned to speak, with the morning light pouring through the kitchen window to make a rainbow of colors on the tile counter top.

In the weeks that followed, as the baby was born and Shanna took her home, no one seemed to understand our pain. Steve's family couldn't see why we would stay away from family gatherings where the baby would be. From their view, we were overreacting. After all, the family still got a new baby. All the gifts they bought were given to the baby just the same. It was only Steve and I who felt the loss. We were left to grieve alone.

After the failed adoption attempt with Shanna, we continued infertility treatments and also tried to find another baby to adopt. So the waiting started again, along with the hoping, the disappointments, the wondering if it would ever happen for us.

"Doesn't anyone care? Doesn't anyone understand?" I cried so many times during those years when I felt abandoned by God and forgotten by him. Little did I know that he really did care. He understood. He had a plan. But I wouldn't find that out for another three years.

By that time infertility treatments had eaten up our savings. Steve had recently lost his job and was now working as a Kelly temp. I was a substitute teacher. And, to top it off, we'd sold our house and moved to a rental in a nearby town. In other words, not only was the possibility of continuing treatments looking grim, but we weren't exactly what an adoption agency or birth mom would be looking for. All my hopes for a baby came crumbling down around me. I felt there was no way I'd ever be a mom.

But just when life looked the bleakest, another call came.

I was working a Christmas job at the mall when my friend Sally handed me the phone. "It's Steve," she said. "He says it's important."

A dozen red and green ribbons in my hand, I took the receiver with the other. "Hey, hon, we're pretty busy here right now," I said, as another customer approached my booth.

"Would you like a brand-new baby boy?" Steve blurted out.

"Call me back in ten minutes."

"Oh, okay."

I hung up the phone, then stopped. Did Steve just say what I thought he said? Something about a baby? I grabbed the phone again, turning to my customer. "I'm sorry, I need to make a call. Sally will help you." I quickly dialed home again and waited. The phone rang and rang and rang. Finally I hung up.

The next ten minutes dragged by like an eighteen-wheeler going up a steep grade. Finally the phone rang. I snatched it up. "Steve, is that you?"

Steve laughed. "Did you even hear me the first time I called?"

"Not really. Did you say something about a baby?"

"A baby boy. Shelley from next door called about him this morning."

"Tell me more."

"Well, his mother's a fourteen-year-old rape victim who chose to go ahead with the pregnancy and place the baby up for adoption. Shelley's sister was going to adopt him, but she just found out she's pregnant, so Shelley called us."

I was silent.

"Did you hear me? They want to know if we want to adopt the baby."

"Are you sure it's for real this time?"

"Pretty sure. Shelley says so."

My mind spun around the possibility. *A baby? For me? For us?* I cleared my throat. "You said yes, didn't you?"

Steve laughed again. "I said I'd talk to you, but I was sure you'd agree."

"Of course I do!" The customer at the counter gave me a strange look as my voice raised an octave.

"Well, the mother's in the hospital tonight and is supposed to be induced tomorrow morning. I'm five minutes from there now. Can you meet me?"

"I'll be there in ten minutes." I slammed down the receiver, grabbed my coat, and headed for the parking lot. "I gotta go!" I yelled to Sally. "I won't be back until tomorrow. Cover for me?"

"Sure," she shouted back. "But this better be good."

"It is!"

I reached the hospital in record time, met Steve, and hurried up to the room. The moment I met Missy, I knew she was a special girl. She looked up at us from the bed and smiled. "So you're the family Shelley told me about?" She extended her hand. I took it in my own. "I'm so glad my baby's going to such a good home." She closed her eyes.

I leaned over and squeezed her hand tighter. "Thank you. You don't know how much this means to us."

Her eyes, deep brown and innocent, opened and looked up into mine. "It was the only way I could think of to make good come from the awful thing that happened to me."

I nodded, as any words I would have said clogged behind the lump in my throat.

For two hours we sat with her and talked, until visiting hours were over. "Come back tomorrow," she called as a nurse showed us out of the room. "You'll want to be here when he's born."

That night was the longest of my life. The next morning we went to the hospital and sat in the waiting room. Casey was born at eleven minutes to seven that evening. The nurse ushered us into the birthing room.

Missy sat up in the bed with a baby in her arms. Her mother stood beside her. Missy looked from the baby to us. A smile lit her face. "He's perfect," she said. "Healthy and perfect."

I held my breath, fearing what else she might say, hoping for what I had thought was impossible. Slowly she lifted the baby and held him toward me. "My gift to you," she whispered as she placed him in my arms.

At that moment, as I looked into Casey's tiny, scrunched up face, I knew that the tests, the pills, the lunch hours with no lunch were all over. I was immediately enamored and fascinated with the small bundle in my arms and amazed that God and Missy were granting us this precious gift.

When we got home, my sister was waiting for us with packages of onesies, sleepers, blankets, wipes, and over two hundred diapers. The next day friends and family brought over a bassinet, a stroller, a car seat, cans of formula, and all kinds of miscellaneous baby things. By the time we brought Casey home, we had everything we needed.

The next day my parents came to visit. When they'd first heard about Casey, they immediately brought up a dozen objections. *What if they take him away?* *What if she changes her mind?* *What if this turns out like the last one?* They were determined not to get attached until everything was finalized. But as soon as they came through the door and took one look at the tiny baby in my arms, they were instantly transformed into Casey's grandparents.

On the day of my shower for Casey two weeks later, my mother wept when I introduced her to Shelley. She gave her a big hug and said, "Thank you for my grandson!" I was filled with wonder at what God had done for all of us.

Then two years and ten months later another call came, and to make a long story short, a baby daughter joined our family.

We're in our late forties now, and the kids are eleven and eight. Today

I can look back on the heartache of infertility and see that through all the pain, through all the disappointments, God hadn't forgotten us. Despite my doubts and questions, God knew what he was doing. And though I may not have believed it when we were going through the tests, procedures, miscarriages, and failed adoption, God's plan was in operation. In fact, everything turned out just right.

TWENTY-THREE

THE SECOND BEDROOM ON THE RIGHT

Catherine, age 48

I always knew the second bedroom on the right would be filled with children's laughter. What I didn't know was that the children wouldn't be mine.

Rick and I bought our house in Thousand Oaks specifically because it was large enough to hold the family we planned to have. With rooms that could be changed from offices to nurseries, and a backyard large enough for a swing set and a playhouse, it was perfect for the large family we dreamed of. And what dreams we had! A little curly-haired girl who'd look up at her mommy with big blue eyes. A boy who would run his play truck over the carpet and make *vroom, vroom* sounds just like Daddy once did. A cooing baby who'd grasp our fingers in a chubby fist while learning to giggle for the first time. We had such love to share with these children of our dreams, such hopes for their futures, such bright plans for the family we just knew God would give us.

But a year passed, then two, then three, and still the second bedroom on the right remained empty.

Soon our dreams shivered and shrunk beneath waves of fear we never thought we'd have to face. Lunches out were replaced with appointments at the infertility clinic. Shopping sprees gave way to tests and procedures and questions meant to uncover the "why" behind our failure to conceive. But the why escaped us. Months of Clomid ended in failure. Temperature charts and ovulation kits yielded no results. And every month I hoped and prayed and then wept when the pregnancy test showed negative again.

Eventually the doctor scheduled a hysterosalpingography. I still remember the day I went in for the procedure. "You have a great chance of getting pregnant right after the HSG," explained the doctor. "This might be the month."

My hopes soared. By the end of the year I could have a baby, a smiling bundle of joy who would drive the fears from me and replace them with the peace of answered prayer. I could imagine it so clearly, clearly enough to convince myself it would be true, clearly enough to resurrect the plans Rick and I had tried to suppress during the previous years of prayer and failure. If she was a girl, I'd name her Grace. If he was a boy, he would be called Andrew. I'd buy that little plastic pool and clean up the cradle I'd picked up at a garage sale three years before. And I knew just how I would decorate the nursery. Green and yellow curtains dotted with baby animals. Noah's ark painted on the back wall. Teddy bears lining the shelves on the left. To the right, a tall bookshelf filled with dozens and dozens of my favorite children's books. It would be perfect. Just like I'd always dreamed.

Then two weeks into my cycle I ovulated right on schedule. Everything looked so good. Two more weeks passed and my monthly period didn't come. My hopes raced higher. One day late, then two.

"I think I'm pregnant," I whispered to Rick.

"Are you sure?" he whispered back.

I smiled. "Not yet. I'll give it a few more days, then I'll get a pregnancy test." But I was confident that I was pregnant. God had finally answered our prayers. And I would be careful to give him all the glory for the baby I hoped was growing inside me. I hugged my arms to my chest. What a testimony I would have at church. What a story to tell at Bible study.

My excitement grew as I visited my local grocery store and saw that they were having a sale on Dr. Seuss books. Surely this was God's way of telling me that I should start filling those nursery bookshelves with the stories I loved. So I decided to buy one book for every day my period was late. *The Cat in the Hat, Green Eggs and Ham, One Fish, Two Fish . . ., How the Grinch Stole Christmas*, each placed neatly on the bookshelf in the second bedroom on the right. Then, the very day I purchased a pregnancy test, it started. That time of month. I couldn't believe it. There would be no baby after all. Disappointment squeezed my heart in a grip so tight that I felt it would crush the life from me. And the disappointment didn't end there. It continued for months and years to come, as time brought me closer to the realization that the second bedroom would never be a nursery.

Now, as I stood outside that bedroom, I remembered it all, the pain of longings unfulfilled, the doubts, the loss of our dreams for a family, a loss that I had grieved as deeply as the death of a loved one.

But on this day, the second bedroom was not empty. A short table ringed with eight little chairs stood in the center of the room. A whiteboard hung on the back wall, and the shelves that I had planned for children's books were filled with crayons, glue, and construction paper for vacation Bible school.

In a moment the doorbell rang, and the house began to fill with children—fifty-five kids in all. By twos and threes they came, chattering as they found their way to the different areas that I had set up for classrooms.

I smiled as I watched them and listened to their eager voices. There was little Katy Ann, who just last week had looked up at me with round brown eyes and said, "I want Jesus to live in my heart, too." She still glowed with the childlike joy of discovering Jesus for her very own. Behind her were Jimmy, John, and Nathan, three sons of a single mother whose Grandma brought them to VBS to learn about God. They were discussing the latest video game in loud whispers. Beyond them Brianna, with a Bible tucked under one arm, trotted toward the stairs. Two months ago she had lost her father in a car accident. Her easy smile still had not returned. My gaze then traveled to Tom and Tim, the twins whose parents recently divorced. Entangled in a nasty custody battle, these once boisterous boys were now strangely quiet. Only in VBS, it seemed, could they put aside their troubles and remember how to be kids again. As I looked around the house, the one we had purchased with our own children in mind, I began to get a glimpse of God's special plan for our lives. So many needs, so many hurts were held in the hearts of the children who came to our vacation Bible school. And God had brought them all to my home, knowing that here they'd find the love their hearts longed for.

Slowly I walked around the house, peeking into one room, then the next. In the living room, the eight- to ten-year-olds were reading the story of blind Bartimaeus. In the dining room, the toddlers were busy building the Tower of Babel with brightly colored blocks. I turned and chuckled as Timmy pulled a block from the bottom of one wall, causing the structure to tumble around him. Then I heard it, the sound of laughter from the second bedroom on the right. And that's when I knew God had blessed me after all. Even though he had never given us children of our own, he did give us a houseful of children to whom we could minister, to whom we made a difference. It wouldn't have been our first choice, this life filled with children not our own, but it wasn't a bad life. Seeing and hearing all these children helped me to understand that. It helped me to realize that God hadn't forgotten us or our love for children. He had his plans, different from our own, but not as desolate as I had once feared.

Sometimes I still wonder what it would have been like to have our own children. Sometimes it still hurts. But during those times, I remember all that God has given me, all the children he has allowed me to love.

A few days ago Rick and I visited my sister's home. Her three children played on the living room floor, while we sipped iced tea and heard all about how Rachel was learning to read, how Matthew went potty on his own for the first time, and how Sarah had won the spelling bee at school last week. On the way home I asked Rick, "Do you wish we'd had children?"

He glanced at me and smiled. "Sure," he said. "That's why we tried for so long. But this is the life God has given us. I'm happy in it, aren't you?"

I paused as I considered his question. "Yes, I am," I finally said. And, surprisingly enough, I meant it. I really did.

TWENTY-FOUR

A PROMISE KEPT

Tami, age 54

I don't believe that every whim is a word from the Lord or every hope is a promise from him. But on that day I knew I'd heard from God. It was a cloudy morning, as overcast as my doubt-filled heart. Glen and I had been married for four years and had been trying to get pregnant for three.

For as long as I could remember, I'd wanted children. I was the oldest in a family of six kids. I helped my mom raise my younger brothers and sisters, all the while dreaming of when I would grow up and have babies of my own. So, after three years of trying, I couldn't believe that I might not have children. I cried out to the Lord, begging him for mercy, for the family I desired.

And on that cloudy day I felt God speak to my heart. *"You will be a mother, Tami. Wait on me."*

So I waited, trusting in the promise of God, believing that any month now I would find myself pregnant. But as the years went by and pregnancy remained elusive, I wondered if I'd really heard from God after all. I tried giving up the dream, laying it on the altar, and walking away. "I guess it's just not going to happen," I'd tell myself. "It's time to get on with my life." Yet the promise wouldn't die in my heart. No matter what I did, there was always a part of me that still waited to be a mother.

Then, after fifteen years of living with infertility, my heart started breaking all over again. The desire for children once more washed over me as strongly as it had so many years before. I approached my husband and said, "Honey, with everything I have in me, I've tried to lay this aside, but I think the Lord is bringing it back. I know you're happy without children, but I'm not. God just won't take the desire from my heart."

Glen nodded. "I understand. Maybe we should talk about adoption."

"Really? You'd consider that?" I asked.

"For you, I will. I love you, Tami. If a child is what you need to be happy, then I'm willing to be a father."

When Glen said that, I felt the love of God filling me. I knew Glen had no desire for children. He'd grown up with an alcoholic father, with no positive male role models in his life, and so had decided that he never wanted to be a dad himself. Yet now he was willing to change his entire life to meet my need. It was a totally unselfish act, and through it God showed me what his love is all about. Over the next months he used Glen's sacrifice to heal my own sense of worthlessness and to show me, in an intimate and practical way, that I have value as an individual. If Glen loved me so much, then God must love me even more.

So we went to an adoption agency, discussed the possibilities, and filled out the application. We were just about ready to schedule our first home visit when Glen came to me and said, "Tami, you know I'm willing to go through with this, if it's what you want. But somehow I just don't think this is right."

My heart sank. *Oh no, this can't be happening. It just can't.* With some sadness, I again went to God. And again I felt him speak to me. *"Tami,"* he said, *"you can continue this process and in six months you'll have a baby in your arms. But you will know that you fulfilled your own desires rather than allowing* me *to fulfill your desires. You must choose—your way, or my way."*

His words brought tears to my eyes. He knew how much I wanted a baby. And he wouldn't remove the desire from my heart. Yet now he was asking me to turn aside from a legitimate way to meet that desire. He was telling me that I must wait—again.

So again I laid my heart on the altar of his will and prayed that God would somehow heal my pain, somehow keep the promise he had given me so long ago.

More time passed. Glen celebrated his fiftieth birthday, and we began to learn to give our love away to other people's children, because it didn't look like we'd ever have any of our own.

In time I came to understand that I needed to stop holding back from living my life to its fullest because I kept hoping for what wasn't happening. So I quit living in the waiting mode and decided to live my life without always thinking, *Maybe this year I'll have a miracle pregnancy, or maybe someone will call and give us a child, or maybe . . .*

In those years I learned that there was a step beyond accepting my situation. That step was embracing the will of God, trusting him and his love for me so completely that I could let go of my plans in order to embrace his.

I was content now with my life, knowing that God had chosen this path for me, that he loved me and had not forgotten me. Yet all the while God's promise stayed with me, even though it seemed that it would never be fulfilled. In my prayers, I would say to God, "I'm no longer going to worry about feeling like a mother and not having any children. In my heart, I am a mother. That's who I am. It's now up to you to give me the child you promised. I just want you to know, I'm still waiting."

Then ten years later it happened. No, I didn't get pregnant, but God kept his promise.

I was in charge of the women's retreat for our church. On Saturday night I gave an altar call at the end of the service. I stood at the microphone and said, "Perhaps you're struggling with a mother-daughter relationship and you need prayer. If so, I invite you to come forward. And if someone is out there who'd like to pray for these women, you come up, too, and pray for them."

I began to think the service was a failure, because hardly anyone responded. But then one young woman came forward, winding her way among the lace-covered tables to kneel at the left side of the altar. I'd seen her at church before, and maybe spoken to her a time or two in the foyer, but I didn't really know her or even remember her name. Then a friend came up and prayed for her. After a few moments I closed the service, and the ladies went to have cookies and ice cream. Still the young woman remained at the altar, although now she knelt alone. I sighed, and said, "I guess I'd better go and pray for her."

I reached out to her and put my arms around her. As soon as I did this, she fell into my arms and started crying. She cried and cried while I prayed for her. Eventually I was quiet, and she raised her head to look me in the eye. "Thank you," she whispered. "Can we talk?"

I glanced out the open doors. Was I needed elsewhere? Should I take the time now to talk further with this young woman? I took a deep breath and decided the ladies could manage without me. I smiled at the dark-haired girl in front of me. "Sure," I answered. "Let's sit down at the first table."

Once we were seated, she began to pour out to me all the pain of her past, her troubled background, her dysfunctional family, the abuse she'd suffered as a child.

"But the worst part," she said, "is that I've never felt as if I had my mother's unconditional love, acceptance, or approval. And I just don't see how that's ever going to change." She looked down at her hands, fidgeting in her lap. "But a moment ago, God did something for me. Something beautiful." She paused.

I reached over and gripped her hand in my own. "Go on. I'm listening."

"When you put your arms around me there at the altar, all of a sudden I felt a mother's unconditional love. I felt God take the broken pieces of the little girl in me and put those pieces back together." She raised her head. "I know this is going to sound weird, but as you prayed for me, it seemed as if God was saying, 'Jenny, this is your mom. I've allowed her to step into that place in your life.'"

I smiled warmly and told her how glad I was that God had ministered to her. Yet her words didn't really penetrate. We talked for a bit longer, then hugged, and she went off to bed, while I headed to the kitchen to help clean up. The next morning the retreat ended.

In Tuesday's mail there was a letter from the young woman. On the envelope, in red ink, it read, *"Please pray about this letter before you open it."* I sighed and set it aside, planning to pray and open it later.

Then Glen came home from work. He saw the letter on the counter and asked, "What's this?"

I put away the plate I was drying and turned toward him. "Oh, there was this woman at the retreat that I prayed with. She said God really ministered to her. It's from her."

"So what does it say?"

"I haven't read it yet."

"Why not?"

I pointed to the envelope. "She says I'm supposed to pray about it first. But I haven't prayed."

Glen snatched up the letter. "Well, I don't need to pray about it. Mind if I look at it?" I shrugged my shoulders, and he slit the top of the envelope and pulled out two sheets of blue-lined notebook paper. As he began to read, a grin formed on his face and he chuckled. "Oh, you're going to like this. You're *really* going to like this." When he finished, he set the letter down on the counter and suggested I pray about it so I could read it. He kissed me on the cheek and headed down the hall to our bedroom.

I dried my hands on the towel and whispered a quick prayer. "Well, Lord, whatever you're doing here, I guess it's okay with me." Then I picked up the letter and read:

Dear Tami,

Before you start reading, I ask that you take a moment to pray about the contents of this letter. I, too, prayed for guidance before writing this. The reason is, I don't want my problems with emotional dependencies to get in the way of what I'm sensing God is saying to me. So, if we both pray, then God might actually hear and work.

I'm not sure where to begin. I realize we don't know each other very well; however, God used you beyond what my simple words can adequately describe. How can I write the extent of all that has been lacking in my life and in my relationship with my mom in the last thirty-one years? How can I begin to comprehend that in a few short minutes in your embrace, God gave me everything I'd hoped and longed for in those thirty-one years?

I've never known a mother's complete and unconditional love like God showed me through you. I've never known the sense of security, acceptance, and belonging like he showed me in you. Through you, I was told I'm okay. I'm loveable. With the security that came through you, for the first time I have a real sense of freedom in being me. Through your obedience, God provided the glue to hold all my broken pieces together for good. From the very moment you hugged me, God began to speak. He said, "Jenny, this is your mother. I'm allowing her to step into your mother's place." At that moment I was overpowered by a love so intense and complete that I know neither the height nor the depth of it. It was at that moment I felt for the first time a mother's love, a mother's love without conditions or expectations, without having to perform or earn that love. For the first time I felt an honest, open, and real love. And for the first time my heart has a concept of what it means to be loved.

I pray that I'm not sounding too much like a needy basket case. May God reveal to your heart what I'm trying to say, because I think I'm failing miserably.

Today as I left the retreat, I hardly drove a mile before God began speaking to me about you. So, as quickly as I could, I pulled over and began to write. But before I share with you what I wrote, there is a Bible verse that has been going through my mind all day. It takes place while

Jesus is hanging on the cross. John 19:26: "When Jesus saw his mother there, and the disciple whom he loved standing nearby, he said to his mother, 'Dear woman, here is your son,' and to the disciple, 'Here is your mother.'" Does Jesus often make such arrangements today? Does he make physical people into spiritual families? Is this a confirmation of what God spoke to me last night or is this my neediness trying to hang on to what God did through you? I can't say for sure, 100 percent, that I know the answer. All I do know is that in my five-year walk out of lesbianism I have been waiting for the moment of healing that came last night.

So, again, I thank you for your obedience to him, and to you I dedicate the following: There are women who become mothers by choosing to have a child. There are women who become mothers by choosing to raise someone else's child. And there are special women who become mothers because a child chooses them.

Tami, if you'll have me, I choose you.

Love,
Jenny

By the time I finished reading, my cheeks were wet with tears. I called to Glen, and he came out of the bedroom. "Told you so," he whispered with a smile. "Do you want to pray about this together now?"

I nodded. "You first."

So Glen prayed, and I prayed. Then we called Jenny and said, "Welcome to the family."

After that Jenny came over to see me every day for almost two years. We'd talk and pray and often have lunch together. During that time, God restored in her life those things that she had missed while growing up. And God restored to me what I had missed all those years when I was a mother without children. God had finally given me my child. And he had given her a mother who loved her without reserve.

One day when I was looking back in my journal, I found an entry from five years earlier. At that time, I'd written about how God was prompting me to pray for my child even though I didn't have one. But I did know that God had made me a mother, even if I didn't know where my kids were, or if they'd ever be on this Earth. So I started praying without knowing if I was praying for some little kid, a teenager, or a baby who would someday come into my life. In my mind's eye, I pictured a girl with dark hair and wide brown eyes. For several weeks I prayed that God would be with her, minister to her, and lead her to Christ.

When I shared those journal entries with Jenny, her eyes grew round with surprise. "That's just when I was making my decision to walk away from lesbianism and instead walk with the Lord," she said, then smiled. "You were praying for me right then when I needed it the most. Wow, God is awesome!"

A year and a half later Jenny was ministering to a couple of other girls who had recently come to know Christ and were struggling to leave the lesbian lifestyle. Rachel was one of the girls.

One day when Rachel was at home, she sensed God saying to her, "You get out of this relationship now. Right now. This is your last chance." So Rachel walked out the door. She had no place to go, no resources, nothing. She camped in the woods for a few days and didn't know what she was going to do next. When Jenny told us about her, Glen and I said, "If she needs a place to stay for a little while, she's welcome to come here."

That Sunday afternoon Rachel walked in our front door with a cooler in her hand, and she's been here ever since. She became daughter number two.

Now four years after Jenny came into my life, and two and a half years after Rachel, it's amazing what God has done. The girls and I have a very close relationship. Everybody at church calls them my daughters. And I know without a doubt that they are the children God intended us to have. I never could have imagined that he would keep his promise in this way, but I'm glad he did. I love these girls. I'm their mom, and they're my kids. They always will be.

Of course, there are still days when I avoid the new baby at church.

Sometimes I'm just not up to it, even now after all these years. And I still don't volunteer for the nursery. But most of the time I'm okay with babies who are not my own, and I'm finding more and more that I don't mind as much, that I'm happy with how God has worked in my life.

It took almost thirty years for him to fulfill his promise to me. In that time he taught me how to live each day he gives me, to use what I have and who I am, not what I don't have and who I'm not. He taught me to embrace his plan for my life. And he taught me that he is faithful to his promises, even when they don't turn out the way I expect. For that I'll always be grateful.

"Sing, O barren woman, you who never bore a child; burst into song, shout for joy, you who were never in labor; because more are the children of the desolate woman than of her who has a husband," says the LORD. "Enlarge the place of your tent, stretch your tent curtains wide, do not hold back; lengthen your cords, strengthen your stakes. For you will spread out to the right and to the left; your descendants will dispossess nations and settle in their desolate cities" (Isaiah 54:1–3).

Top Survival Tips From Fellow Travelers on the Road of Infertility

Be as informed as possible during your journey with infertility. Doctors don't always have the answers! Research your condition online, but be careful to get your information from reputable sites.

—Lori

Decide your limits (morally, physically, spiritually, financially) before you go for treatment. Put them in writing and share them with your doctor. This will help you stick to your limits when the pressure is on.

—Julie

Don't take everything others say to heart. People will say the most awful, stupid, hurtful things. Expect it, and remember: they (like all of us) are doing the best they can.

—Roseanne

Make sure you understand your insurance coverage and the state laws that apply to coverage of fertility treatments.

—*Michael*

If you're not happy with your doctor, change right away. You need to be understood, be able to ask questions, and not feel threatened or challenged.

—*Jane*

Find support. Your family and friends are important, but they can't replace the value of sharing with other couples who are facing the same fight against infertility. Seek out support groups in your church, community, and on the Internet.

—*Jennifer*

Don't let life pass you by while you are waiting to become a parent. It would be better to cancel plans at the last minute than to let opportunities to enjoy your life and your spouse slip away while you wait.

—*Robin*

Laugh when you want to laugh and cry when you want to cry.

—*Jane*

Give yourself the freedom to grieve. The inability to have a child is a loss. It's okay, even healthy, to grieve that loss. Don't allow people to stop the process by telling you to stop making a fuss.

—*Cathy*

Try to have your husband or another support person with you at doctor visits. You never know when you might receive upsetting news, and it helps to have someone there to comfort you.

—*Kari*

If your marriage suffers because of infertility, get help early! My husband and I found that our infertility problems were tearing us apart. Getting professional help was the best thing we've ever done for our marriage.

—*Heather*

Be selective when telling others about your infertility. Many of us have lived to regret making our struggles common knowledge among family and friends.

—Donnie

Take 400–800 milligrams of ibuprofen an hour or so before an HSG or endometrial biopsy. It really helps lessen the discomfort.

—Kari

Don't waste time being treated by a gynecologist who claims to also treat infertility. The only doctors who have the extra years of training in infertility treatments are reproductive endocrinologists. Go straight to the specialist.

—Sandra

Try to rest in the Lord and wait for his timing and will. Remember to enjoy life right now. Take a walk, and see the beauty and the gifts God has bestowed upon you.

—John

Don't feel bad about feeling bad. Infertility is lousy. It's normal to hurt.

—Linda

If you need to stay home from a family gathering, baby shower, or even a birthday party, do it. Don't feel guilty.

—Janet

Hold onto the Lord with all your mind, body, and spirit. Honestly, he's our only hope!

—Kimberly

Remember, this is not a sprint, but a marathon.

—Laurie

Keep a prayer journal to express your hurt and frustrations. And read good books that will help develop your maturity during this tough time.

—Michelle

Remember, there is a bigger picture that we aren't capable of seeing just yet. Though the pain is real and heartbreaking, the rest of the story will be glorious and beyond our comprehension.

—Carol

Unless someone has experienced or is experiencing infertility, don't pay attention to their clichés or simple answers.

—Dave

Include your husband in the grieving process. Open up to each other regarding what each of you are going through.

—Jane

See a fertility counselor if you can. This wonderful woman kept me from losing my head.

—Nina

The dreams have shattered, but not the spirit. Allow God to comfort and support you.

—Jane

Consider infertility like other trials we face in life—know God has allowed it (Job 1:6–12); don't be surprised by it (1 Peter 4:12); and remember that it's working in you an "eternal glory that far outweighs them all" (2 Corinthians 4:16–18).

—Erica

WHERE TO FIND HELP

The following are Christian ministries that provide help, support, and/or information to those experiencing infertility:

STEPPING STONES

% Bethany Christian Services
901 Eastern Avenue NE
P.O. Box 294
Grand Rapids, MI 49501–0294
Phone: (616) 224–7488
Fax: (616) 224–7593
E-mail: Step@bethany.org
www.bethany.org/step

Stepping Stones is a bimonthly donation-supported Christian newsletter offering hope, encouragement, and support to infertile couples.

HANNAH'S PRAYER MINISTRIES

P.O. Box 5016
Auburn, CA 95604–5016
Phone: (775) 852–9202
E-mail: Hannahs@Hannah.org
www.hannah.org

Hannah's Prayer Ministries is a Christian support network for couples facing fertility challenges, including infertility or the death of a baby at any time from conception through early infancy. Their Web site allows you to connect with pen pals and read back issues of newsletters, and also provides links and contact information for other organizations dealing with infertility or the loss of a child.

LADIES IN WAITING

% Julie Donahue
P.O. Box 5304
Modesto, CA 95352
E-mail: LadeNWaitn@aol.com
http://members.aol.com/ladenwaitn

Ladies in Waiting is an e-mail support group for married Christian women facing infertility.

The following are secular organizations that may be helpful to those experiencing infertility:

RESOLVE

1310 Broadway
Somerville, MA 02144
Phone: (617) 623–0744

E-mail: resolveinc@aol.com

http://www.resolve.org

Resolve is a national organization that provides timely, compassionate support and information, through advocacy and public education, to individuals who are experiencing infertility issues.

THE INTERNATIONAL COUNCIL ON INFERTILITY INFORMATION DISSEMINATION, INC. (INCIID)

P.O. Box 6836

Arlington, VA 22206

Executive Director: Nancy P. Hemenway (703) 379–9178

Media Inquiries: President Theresa Venet Grant (520) 544–9548

Fax: (703) 379–1593

E-mail: INCIIDinfo@inciid.org

http://www.inciid.org

INCIID (pronounced "inside") is a nonprofit organization committed to providing the most current information regarding the diagnosis, treatment, and prevention of infertility and pregnancy loss.

CHILD OF MY DREAMS

http://www.childofmydreams.com

Child of My Dreams provides online information and advice for people facing the challenges of infertility and adoption. Resources include: medical information on the causes, cures, and costs of infertility; information on all types of adoptions; how-to guides on forms, home visits, and international adoptions; professional fertility and adoption experts who can answer questions directly through message boards or during live speakers events.

TRUSTWORTHY WISDOM
FOR SEASONS OF CHANGE

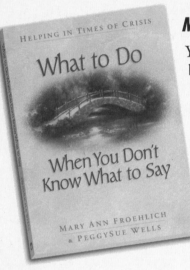

Meaningful Ways to Help in Times of Crisis

Your desire to help those in need is sincere, but sometimes you're unsure how, finding yourself at a loss for what to say to provide encouragement. This collection of stories of people touching the lives of others provides you with practical and doable answers to the question "How can I help?"

What to Do When You Don't Know What to Say
by Mary Ann Froehlich and PeggySue Wells

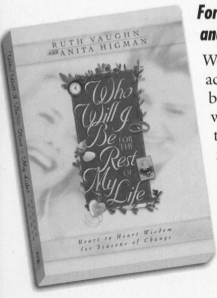

For Women Looking Toward the Changes and Challenges Ahead

Women of all ages wonder if they can accomplish or experience all their dreams, but rarely feel free to share their concerns with others. These two authors did, though, and you'll be a part of their remarkable correspondence—a season of sharing that began on Anita's fortieth birthday.

Who Will I Be For the Rest of My Life
by Anita Higman and Ruth Vaughn